the contented
vegetarian

the contented
vegetarian

Over 100 tempting and nutritious step-by-step recipes
for quick, easy and healthy dining

matthew drennan and annie nichols

southwater

This edition is published by Southwater

Southwater is an imprint of Anness Publishing Ltd
Hermes House, 88–89 Blackfriars Road, London SE1 8HA
tel. 020 7401 2077; fax 020 7633 9499
www.southwaterbooks.com; info@anness.com

© Anness Publishing 1997, 2004

UK agent: The Manning Partnership Ltd, 6 The Old Dairy, Melcombe Road, Bath BA2 3LR;
tel. 01225 478444; fax 01225 478440; sales@manning-partnership.co.uk

UK distributor: Grantham Book Services Ltd, Isaac Newton Way,
Alma Park Industrial Estate, Grantham, Lincs NG31 9SD;
tel. 01476 541080; fax 01476 541061; orders@gbs.tbs-ltd.co.uk

North American agent/distributor: National Book Network,
4501 Forbes Boulevard, Suite 200, Lanham, MD 20706;
tel. 301 459 3366; fax 301 429 5746; www.nbnbooks.com

Australian agent/distributor: Pan Macmillan Australia, Level 18,
St Martins Tower, 31 Market St, Sydney, NSW 2000;
tel. 1300 135 113; fax 1300 135 103; customer.service@macmillan.com.au

New Zealand agent/distributor: David Bateman Ltd, 30 Tarndale Grove, Off Bush Road,
Albany, Auckland; tel. (09) 415 7664; fax (09) 415 8892

A CIP catalogue record for this book is available from the British Library.

Publisher: Joanna Lorenz
Senior Cookery Editor: Linda Fraser
In-house Editor: Margaret Malone
Designer: Brian Weldon
Photographers: Karl Adamson, Edward Allwright, James Duncan and Amanda Heywood
Recipes: Matthew Drennan and Annie Nichols
Additional Recipes: Shirley Gill, Carole Handslip and Steven Wheeler
Stylists: Madeleine Brehaut and Hilary Guy

Previously published as *Vegetarian Entertaining*

1 3 5 7 9 10 8 6 4 2

For all recipes, quantities are given in both metric and imperial
measures, and, where appropriate, measures are also given in standard
cups and spoons. Follow one set, but not a mixture, because they are
not interchangeable.

CONTENTS

INTRODUCTION

Today, vegetarian food is a familiar part of everyday cuisine. The notion that vegetarian dishes are uninspiring, heavy and dull has long been dispelled. For many of us, vegetarian food is the perfect solution when quick, light, mid-week standbys are needed. *Vegetarian Entertaining*, however, provides the home cook with a host of delectable ideas for entertaining, with recipes suitable for every occasion from informal relaxed meals to more sumptuous events.

With the growth of vegetarianism we have discovered the joy of cooking with foods such as grains, pulses and vegetables, and *Vegetarian Entertaining* demonstrates how easy it can be to produce a complete vegetarian lunch or dinner menu that looks good, tastes delicious and is also simple and easy to prepare. All the recipes combine freshly prepared produce with staples from the store cupboard or freezer and utilize the proliferation of new and exotic herbs and spices now readily available, making it possible to create exciting and imaginative dishes with ease.

The secret of success when entertaining is to make sure you have all the ingredients and necessary equipment before you begin. Advice on stocking the store cupboard and what constitutes a survival kitchen is given on the next few pages. Decide on your menu as early as possible, and work out what preparations can be done beforehand. The menu planner section provides some useful suggestions for combining appropriate starters, main courses, salads and desserts. Master the 'all hands on deck' method, using the time while one item is cooking to prepare the next, and you may be surprised to discover just how easy it can be to cook a number of dishes and still enjoy the occasion.

So, whether you are entertaining with family and friends or planning a more formal meal, this book shows you how to plan and cook a complete vegetarian menu that is both delicious and easy to prepare – leaving you with more time to spend with your guests. Fully illustrated with step-by-step instructions, *Vegetarian Entertaining* ensures that you will never be short of a perfect and tempting dish for every special occasion.

The Store Cupboard

Your store cupboard should be the backbone of your kitchen. Stock it sensibly and you'll always have the wherewithal to make a tasty, satisfying meal. Begin with the basics and expand as you experiment, buying small quantities where possible and keeping an eye on "use by" dates.

OILS, SAUCES AND CANNED GOODS

Chilli oil
Use this fiery oil sparingly to liven up vegetable stir-fries and similar dishes.

Groundnut oil
This bland-tasting oil will not mask delicate flavours. It is good for deep-frying. Use vegetable or sunflower oil instead, if you prefer.

Olive oil
If you must have only one oil, a good olive oil will suit most purposes (except deep-frying). Extra virgin olive oil is more expensive and best kept for salads.

Sesame oil
Favoured in oriental cooking for its flavour, this rich oil can be used on its own or combined with vegetable oil.

Ghee
This is pure clarified butter. Used extensively in Indian cooking, it is usually sold in blocks or cans.

Black bean sauce
A thick aromatic sauce made from beans, used for marinades and stir-fries.

Passata
This thick sauce is made from sieved tomatoes. It is mainly used in Italian cookery.

Soy sauce
A thin, salty, black liquid made from fermented soya beans. Add a splash at the end of cooking and offer extra at the table.

Sun-dried tomatoes
These deliciously sweet tomatoes, baked in the sun and dried, are sold in bags or in jars, steeped in olive oil.

Tahini paste
Made from ground sesame seeds, this paste is used in Middle Eastern cookery.

Tomato purée
This is a concentrated tomato paste which is sold in cans, jars or tubes. A version made from sun-dried tomatoes is also now available.

Canned pulses
Chick-peas, cannellini beans, green lentils, haricot beans and red kidney beans survive the canning process well. Wash in cold running water and drain well before use.

Canned vegetables
Although fresh vegetables are best for most cooking, some canned products are very useful. Artichoke hearts have a mild sweet flavour and are great for adding to stir-fries, salads, risottos or pizzas. Pimientos are canned whole red peppers, seeded and peeled. Use them for stews and soups, but stick to fresh peppers for anything else as they lack the firmness of bite that is needed for dishes such as stir-fries. Canned tomatoes are an essential ingredient to have in the store cupboard. There is now a very wide range available, whole or chopped, plain or with herbs, spices or other flavourings. Additional useful items to include are ratatouille (make sure it is a good brand, though) and sweetcorn.

chick-peas

tahini paste

tomato purée

golden syrup

red wine

chilli sauce

chopped
tomatoes

chilli
oil

herb vinegar

black olive
paste

sweetcorn

pimientos

white wine
vinegar

ratatouille

kidney beans

lentils

chillies in oil

tahini
paste

plum tomatoes

soy sauce

black bean
sauce

olive
oil

mustard

honey

passata

groundnut
oil

red wine
vinegar

balsamic
vinegar

black olives

salad dressing

ghee

Dry Goods

Assuming your store cupboard already includes flours, sugars and dried fruits, the following items are invaluable for speedy cooking. The list of spices relates specifically to the recipes contained in this book.

Bulgur wheat
This whole wheat grain is steam-dried and cracked before sale, so only needs a brief soaking before use. Keep it cool and dry in the cupboard and it will last for a few months.

Nuts
Buy nuts in small quantities and store in a dry place. Almonds, cashews, peanuts, pecans, pine nuts and walnuts all feature prominently in this book.

Pasta
While fresh pasta is generally preferred, both for flavour and for speed of cooking, the dried product is a very valuable store cupboard ingredient. Spaghetti, noodles (Italian and oriental) and shapes are all useful.

Rice
If you stock only one type of rice, make it basmati, which has a superior flavour and fragrance. A mixture of basmati and wild rice (not a true rice, but the seeds of an aquatic grass) works well.

SPICES

Caraway seeds
Small greenish-brown seeds with a nutty texture and a flavour reminiscent of aniseed or fennel.

Chinese five-spice powder
Made from a mixture of anise pepper, cassia, fennel seed, star anise and cloves, this spice has an enticing aniseed (licorice) flavour.

Garam masala
This is an aromatic mixture of different spices used widely in Indian dishes. It is usually added at the end of cooking.

Ground cardamom
Fragrant, with a spicy undertone, cardamom is used in sweet and savoury dishes.

Ground cinnamon
A sweet fragrant spice ground from the dried rolled inner bark of a tropical tree.

Ground coriander
With a warm savoury aroma, this spice imparts a mildly hot yet sweetish flavour.

Ground cumin
Sweet and pungent, with a unique and distinctive taste.

Ground turmeric
With a somewhat musty flavour and aroma, this spice adds a deep yellow colour to food. It is sometimes used in place of saffron to add colour, although it does not have the same flavour.

Saffron
This is the most expensive spice in the world. It has a pungent scent with a slightly bitter-sweet taste. The threads are crushed and steeped in a little liquid before use.

rice

ground turmeric

ground cumin

caraway s

egg noodles

nuts

penne

bulgur
wheat

pecan nuts

garam
masala

dried chillies

spaghetti

cornflour

mixed spice

black
peppercorns

Chinese five-
spice powder

pine nuts

poppy seeds

chilli
powder

ground
coriander

sea salt

thyme

cumin seed

caster sugar

long grain
rice

granulated
sugar

garlic

Fresh Fruit and Vegetables

Thanks to the amazing range of fresh produce now available, the vegetarian repertoire has expanded enormously. Filled with complex carbohydrates, protein, vitamins and minerals, fresh fruit and vegetables are essential to a healthy vegetarian diet.

Alfalfa sprouts
These crisp, sprouting seeds with a delicious nutty flavour are highly nutritious and rich in protein, fibre, vitamins and minerals.

Baby sweetcorn
These young corn are most delicious when lightly cooked, so are especially suitable for stir-fries.

Broad beans
The plump inner bean is delicious when lightly steamed, and makes a good accompaniment to richly flavoured foods.

Celeriac
This underrated vegetable has a delicious, sweet, celery-like flavour.

Chillies
There are hundreds of varieties of these hot relatives of the capsicum family. They should be treated with caution. When preparing chillies take special care to avoid rubbing your eyes or face as their juices can irritate the skin.

Fennel
A crisp, delicious, sweet aniseed-flavoured vegetable, which can be eaten raw, finely sliced, or cooked. Add a little to vegetable stock for an unusual extra flavouring.

Limes
Fresh and sharp with an intense sour flavour.

Okra
Okra lends a creamy, silky consistency to vegetable dishes.

Patty pan squash
These lovely, scallop-edged baby squash have a similar flavour to courgettes.

Peas
Sweet, tender peas, popped fresh from the pod are unbeatable. Make the most of them when in season.

Pumpkins
There are many different varieties of these members of the gourd family. A thick tough skin belies the fragrant, pale or bright orange flesh within.

Red onions
Mild and sweeter than most onions, their purple flesh makes a pretty addition to any vegetable dish.

Sweet potatoes
The skin of these tubers can be pinkish or brown and the flesh varies from creamy white to yellow or pale orange. Despite its name, this vegetable is not related to the everyday potato. The sweet potato usually has an elongated shape, although some round varieties are available.

Tomatoes
Recent demand for full-flavoured tomatoes means that varieties now abound, from the sweet little cherry tomatoes, to the plump Italian plum and the large beefsteak tomatoes.

Turnips
Sweet, nutty-flavoured turnips range from the walnut-sized baby roots (that are often sold still attached to their green tops) to large mature turnips.

fennel

okra

turnips

celeriac

pumpkin

tomatoes

chilies

broad beans

plum tomatoes

cherry tomatoes

sweet potatoes

peas

alfalfa sprouts

red onions

patty pan squash

limes

baby corn

Pasta, Pulses and Grains

Pasta, pulses and grains all belong to the important complex carbohydrate group. Most are low in fat and contain plenty of vitamins, minerals and dietary fibre.

Aduki beans
A small, reddish brown, shiny bean with a unique strong nutty, sweet flavour.

Arborio rice
One of the best and most commonly available rices to use for risotto.

Basmati rice and brown basmati rice
Harvested from the foothills of the Himalayas with a very distinctive, fragrant aroma.

Black-eyed beans
Sometimes referred to as black-eyed peas, these small beans with a black spot have a savoury flavour and succulent texture.

Bulgur wheat
A whole wheat grain that is steamed-dried and cracked so it only needs brief soaking before use.

Campanelle
A pretty frilled, twisted pasta tube.

Cannellini beans
These look like small white kidney beans and belong to the same family. They have a soft texture when cooked.

Capellini
Known as angel-hair pasta, this is a very fine variety.

Chick-peas
These pale golden-brown, hard peas look rather like small dry hazelnuts. They have a rich nutty flavour.

Couscous
Made from coarse semolina, this lovely soft grain is now produced to need only a brief moistening before use.

Egg noodles
The most common of all oriental noodles, they take only minutes to cook.

Flageolet beans
Pale green, long and slim, these are haricot beans removed from the pod while young. They have a tender texture when cooked.

Haricot beans
These oval cream beans are commonly seen as canned baked beans. A versatile bean with a mild flavour.

Long-grain rice and brown long-grain rice
Long, translucent grains are valued for their nutty flavour.

Oatmeal
Sliced whole oat grain which is graded from pinhead (the coarsest) to medium and fine (medium is shown here). A good source of calcium, potassium and iron.

Pasta bows
The Italian name for this is *farfalle* or 'butterfly', because of its shape.

Penne
Short, tubular pasta shapes, also known as quills.

Polenta
Fine yellow cornmeal, used to make a soft porridge of the same name.

Puy lentils
This superior lentil is prized for its flavour and texture.

Soup pasta
This tiny pasta comes in many different shapes.

Spaghetti
The most popular pasta, it has long, thin strands.

Tagliatelle
Flat, long ribbon noodles. The green version is flavoured with spinach.

Wild rice
Not a true rice but the seed of an aquatic grass. The brown, long grains open when cooked.

spaghetti

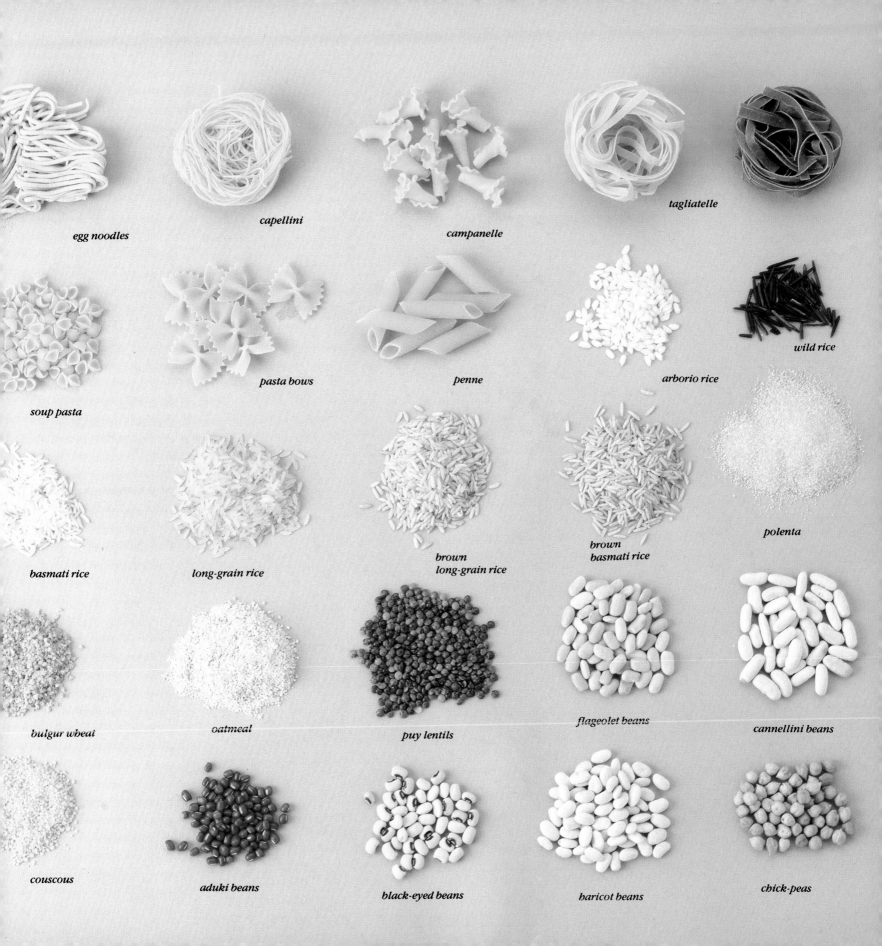

egg noodles

capellini

campanelle

tagliatelle

soup pasta

pasta bows

penne

arborio rice

wild rice

basmati rice

long-grain rice

brown
long-grain rice

brown
basmati rice

polenta

bulgur wheat

oatmeal

puy lentils

flageolet beans

cannellini beans

couscous

aduki beans

black-eyed beans

haricot beans

chick-peas

The Vegetarian Store Cupboard

Although not strictly essential, the ingredients listed here will greatly enhance any vegetarian dish, and are convenient to have on hand when preparing food at the last minute.

Balsamic vinegar
A deliciously smooth, rich, sweet-and-sour flavoured vinegar made in Modena in northern Italy.

Hazelnut oil
A richly flavoured nutty oil. Just a few drops will lift the flavour of a plain salad.

Olive oil
This is high in mono-unsaturated fats and vitamin A. It ranges from the refined pale yellow variety to the rich herbaceous extra-virgin.

Raspberry vinegar
A sweet, light vinegar with the slight tang of raspberries.

Sesame oil
This delicious, rich oil is often used in oriental cuisine as a flavouring rather than as a cooking oil.

Sunflower oil
A mild polyunsaturated oil that is useful for all types of cooking.

Sun-dried tomatoes
A preserved tomato which can be bought either in bags or steeped in olive oil in jars.

Tahini
A paste made from ground sesame seeds, it is widely used in Middle Eastern cooking.

Walnut oil
High in polyunsaturates, this is a delicious nutty oil.

Cheeses and Tofu

Improvements in handling and distribution mean that we are now able to buy a huge range of local and imported cheeses in excellent condition. Tofu, available in various forms, is another valuable source of protein.

Blue cheese
Where a recipe fails to specify a particular blue cheese, use Roquefort if a strong flavour is required and dolcelatte for a milder result.

Camembert
This cheese is made from cow's milk. It has a mild creamy taste with a slight acidic edge that gets milder with age.

Feta
This soft Greek cheese is rindless, white in colour and has a crumbly texture. It is slightly sour, piquant and quite salty to the taste.

Goat's cheese
Fresh goat's cheese is soft and creamy. As it ages, the cheese becomes harder and the flavour intensifies.

Mozzarella
A unique Italian cheese made from cow's milk, mozzarella has a mild, creamy taste and an unusual spongy texture.

Parmesan
A hard cheese from Italy with a wonderful, distinctive flavour. It is usually grated or shaved wafer-thin. Buy it fresh as the ready-grated cheese sold commercially often lacks flavour.

Stilton
An English semi-hard cheese with blue veins, Stilton has a soft moist texture and a strong flavour.

Tofu
This is an unfermented bean curd made from soya beans. It absorbs flavours readily and is frequently marinated before use. Various forms are available, from soft silken tofu to a firm type which can be cubed and sautéed.

Spices and Seasonings

Spices and seasonings are indispensable for enhancing the flavours of foods that might otherwise be bland and lacking in substance.

fennel seeds

star anise

cayenne

ginger

Allspice
This is available both whole and ground and imparts a flavouring that is like a mixture of nutmeg, cinnamon, cloves and pepper.

Caraway
A pungent and aromatic spice that is widely used in German and Austrian cooking.

Cayenne
Ground from small red chillies, it is extremely spicy, and should be used sparingly.

Cinnamon
Cinnamon is a sweet and fragrant spice ground from the dried, rolled inner bark of a tropical tree that is native to Sri Lanka.

Cloves
A strongly aromatic spice with a slightly bitter taste.

Coriander
A sweet, warm aromatic spice that is used extensively in Indian and South-east Asian cooking.

Cumin
A uniquely flavoured spice with a sweetly pungent and very distinctive taste.

Fennel seeds
These seeds have a strong, sweet anise-liquorice flavour.

Ginger
The fresh root has a clean refreshing flavour. Ginger is also available dried and ground.

Green cardamom
The pods should be broken open and the small black seeds ground to fully appreciate the mellow fragrant, slightly spicy aroma.

Juniper berries
These pine-scented, bitter-sweet berries provide the main flavouring of gin.

Lemon grass
A strong clean, refreshing citrus flavouring that is widely used in Thai and Vietnamese cooking.

Nutmeg
A very aromatic spice with a warm, sweet, nutty flavour.

Paprika
The flavour can range from sweet and lightly piquant, to pungent and fiery.

Saffron
This is the most expensive spice in the world, but you need only a tiny amount to flavour and colour any dish.

Star anise
A sweet, pungent liquorice-flavoured spice that is important in Chinese cooking.

Turmeric
Mainly used for its bright yellow colouring, it has a slightly musty taste and aroma.

Yellow mustard seeds
Less pungent than brown or black mustard seeds, they have a sweet, mild piquancy.

green cardamom

ground
cloves

cloves

ground
nutmeg

nutmeg

ground coriander

coriander seeds

ground cumin

cumin
seeds

allspice berries

ground allspice

ground turmeric

ground
cinnamon

cinnamon
sticks

ground ginger

caraway
seeds

juniper berries

yellow mustard seeds

saffron

lemon grass

paprika

Nuts

Nuts provide a healthy source of energy, and are rich in fibre, protein, vitamins B and E and several minerals. However, they are high in fats (though mostly mono- and polyunsaturated) so are usually also high in calories.

Almonds
There are two types, sweet and bitter, the bitter type being poisonous when eaten raw. This delicious nut enriches many dishes and is especially high in protein.

Brazil nuts
As the name would suggest, these nuts originate from the Brazilian Amazon. The high oil content means that these nuts quickly turn rancid.

Chestnuts
Not to be confused with the horse-chestnut, these softer textured nuts are low in fat and high in carbohydrates. They can be bought fresh, canned (whole or puréed), vacuum-packed and dried.

Hazelnuts
These wonderfully aromatic sweet nuts add flavour to both sweet and savoury dishes. Roasting adds more flavour.

Peanuts
Not strictly a true nut, these most popular of nuts have a distinctive flavour and are rich in protein.

Pecans
A native of the USA, these are sweet and richly flavoured nuts similar to walnuts.

Pine nuts
These soft, creamy coloured nuts are found at the base of a species of pine cone. They have a delicate flavour.

Pistachios
These are richly flavoured with a bright green colouring.

Walnuts
The most versatile of all nuts, walnuts impart a rich full flavour.

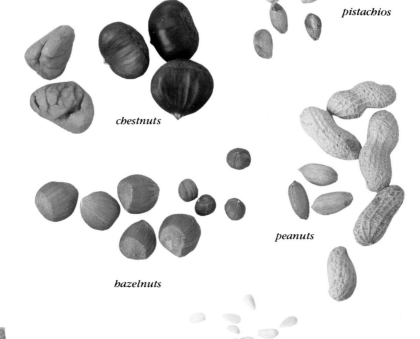

brazil nuts

chestnuts

pistachios

almonds

hazelnuts

peanuts

pine nuts

walnuts

Flours

Flour can be ground from grains, cereals, seeds, nuts and even roots and tubers.

Buckwheat flour
A non-wheat flour, ground from the seed of a plant that is related to rhubarb. It has a strong nutty flavour and is rich in vitamins A and B, calcium and carbohydrate.

White flour
This contains 75 per cent or less of the wheat grain so is not as nutritious as wholemeal flour.

Wholemeal flour
Ground from the entire whole grain it is rich in protein, vitamins and fibre, so is highly nutritious.

white flour

wholemeal flour

buckwheat flour

Seeds

Seeds provide a rich source of protein, fibre, vitamins, minerals and starch.

Poppy seeds
These mild, sweet seeds come from the opium poppy, but are free from narcotic properties.

Pumpkin seeds
From the vegetable of the same name, these flat green seeds have a light, distinctive flavour and are rich in zinc, protein and iron.

Sesame seeds
These tiny, light brown or creamy coloured seeds have a mild, sweet nutty flavour and are rich in protein and calcium.

Sunflower seeds
These seeds have a distinctive flavour and they are rich in protein, fibre, iron and calcium.

pumpkin seeds

poppy seeds

sunflower seeds

sesame seeds

Equipment

Stocking up on every item in your local cookware shop will not make you a better cook, but some basic items are definitely worth investing in.

A few good saucepans in various sizes and with tight-fitting lids are a must. Heavy-based and non-stick pans are best. A large non-stick frying pan is invaluable for the quick cook. The food cooks faster when spread over a wider surface area. For the same reason, a good wok is essential. I suggest using a large saucepan or frying pan when the recipe calls for occasional stirring, and a wok for continuous movement, such as stir-frying.

Good quality knives can halve your preparation time, but more importantly, a really sharp knife is safer than a blunt one. You can do yourself a lot of damage if your hand slips when you are pressing down hard with a blunt knife. For basic, day-to-day use choose a good chopping knife, a small vegetable knife and a long serrated bread knife. If possible store knives safely in well-secured slotted racks. Drawer storage is not good for knives as the blades can easily become damaged when they are knocked around. If you do have to keep knives in a drawer, make sure they are stored with their handles towards the front for safe lifting and keep the blades protected in some way. Good sharp knives are essential and indispensable pieces of kitchen equipment, so it is worth taking care of them.

A few of the recipes in this book call for the use of a food processor, which does save time and effort but is not strictly necessary. Other essential pieces of kitchen equipment which almost seem too obvious to mention include chopping boards, a colander, a sieve, a grater, a whisk and some means of extracting citrus juice, be this a squeezer or a juicer.

For the cook who likes to cook speedily and efficiently, where you store your equipment is an important factor to consider. I use my cooker as the pivot around which most of the action takes place. Pots, pans, whisks, spoons and strainers hang conveniently overhead within easy reach, a chopping board is on an adjacent work surface and ceramic pots hold a variety of wooden spoons, spatulas, ladles, scissors, peelers and other kitchen utensils, again all within easy reach.

wooden spatula

ladle

scissors

knives and peelers

vegetable knife

bread knife

whisks

draining
spoon

grater

serving
spoon

chopping
board

colander

saucepans

wok

frying pan

TECHNIQUES

Once mastered, the techniques described here will help you to prepare vegetables speedily and with less waste, to produce better results with ease.

Peeling and Seeding Tomatoes
A simple and efficient way of preparing tomatoes.

1 Use a sharp knife to cut a small cross on the bottom of the tomato.

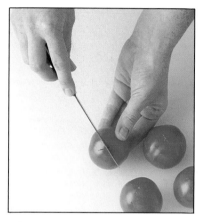

2 Turn the tomato over and cut out the core.

3 Immerse the tomato in boiling water for 10–15 seconds, then transfer to a bowl of cold water using a slotted spoon.

4 Lift out the tomato and peel (the skin should be easy to remove).

5 Cut the tomato in half crosswise and squeeze out the seeds.

6 Use a large knife to cut the peeled tomato into strips, then chop across the strips to make dice.

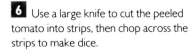

Chopping Onions

Uniform-sized dice make cooking easy. This method can't be beaten.

1 Peel the onion. Cut it in half with a large knife and set it cut-side down on a board. Make lengthwise vertical cuts along the onion, cutting almost but not quite through to the root.

2 Make 2 horizontal cuts from the stalk and towards the root, but not through it.

3 Cut the onion crosswise to form small, even dice.

Slicing Onions

Use thin slices for sautéeing or to flavour oils for stir-frying, or use sweet onion slices in salads.

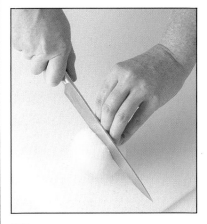

1 Peel the onion. Cut it in half with a large knife and set it cut-side down on a chopping board.

2 Cut out a triangular piece of the core from each half.

3 Cut across each half in vertical slices.

Shredding Cabbage

This method is useful for coleslaws, pickled cabbage or any cooked dish.

1 Use a large knife to cut the cabbage into quarters.

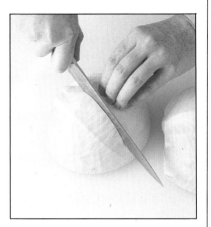

2 Cut out the core from each quarter.

3 Slice across each quarter to form fine, even shreds.

Cutting Carrot Julienne

Thin julienne strips of any vegetable make decorative accompaniments, or can be used in stir-fries.

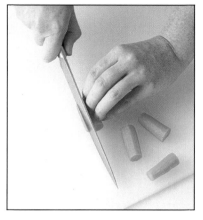

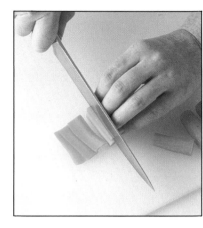

1 Peel the carrot and use a large knife to cut it into 5 cm/2 in lengths. Cut a thin sliver from one side of each piece so that it sits flat on the board.

2 Cut into thin lengthwise slices.

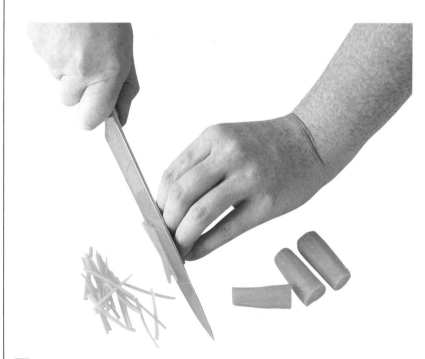

3 Stack the slices and cut through them to make fine strips.

Chopping Fresh Ginger

Fresh ginger imparts a clean, refreshing taste. Follow the instructions to chop finely.

1 Break off small knobs of ginger from the main root and peel.

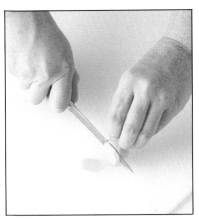

2 Slice lengthwise and cut into strips.

3 Cut across the strips to form small, even dice.

Chopping Chillies

Fresh chillies must be handled with care. Always work in a well-ventilated area and keep away from your eyes.

1 Cut the chilli in half lengthwise and remove the core and seeds.

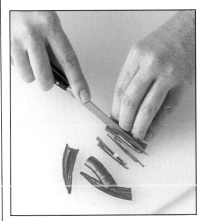

2 Cut it into lengthwise strips.

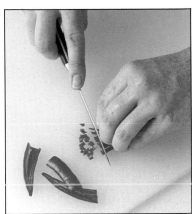

3 Cut across the strips to form small, even dice.

Make a Meal of It

The recipes in this book have been specially chosen as they can be served alone with a simple side order of pasta, rice or potatoes, or they can easily be combined together to form delicious menus, perfect for entertaining. The ease and speed of preparation that is common to them all, makes these dishes the perfect choice for entertaining, as they provide the cook more time to enjoy the company instead of being confined to the kitchen. On the following pages you can choose to combine favourite main course dishes of your choice with the simple-to-make starters and desserts featured, or select from the complete menus provided featuring appropriate dishes for every stage of the meal.

STARTERS

Lightly poached asparagus with crème fraîche and lemon.

Warm focaccia bread accompanied with olive oil, salt crystals and black olives.

Grilled cherry tomatoes served with salad and basil leaves, drizzled with a little dressing.

Crudités of celery, carrot, baby sweetcorn and mange-touts served with mayonnaise with a little pesto stirred through.

Thin slices of French bread, topped with tapenade (black olive paste) and mozzarella, then grilled and served hot.

Ready-made houmus and tzatziki served as dips with strips of warm pitta bread and black olives.

Chopped fresh tomatoes and onion flavoured with chopped fresh coriander and served with poppadums.

DESSERTS

Slices of sticky ginger cake warmed through in the microwave and served with a little golden syrup and cream.

Fresh summer berries, sprinkled with Kirsch and vanilla sugar, served with crème fraîche or natural yogurt.

Sweetened whipped cream flavoured with passion fruit and served on banana slices. Add amaretti biscuits for contrast.

A slice of Swiss roll topped with a scoop of ice cream, covered in stiff meringue and grilled until golden.

Banana slices and orange segments topped with a little apricot jam, wrapped in foil and baked in a hot oven for 10 minutes. Serve with cream.

Fresh blackberries crushed lightly with a fork and gently folded into softly whipped cream. Add a drizzle of Cassis (optional) and sugar to taste.

Brandy snap baskets filled with raspberries and peach slices, topped with a swirl of cream and a sprig of mint.

Ripe plums, halved, sprinkled with brandy and filled with mascarpone cheese. The plums are topped with chopped nuts and demerara sugar then grilled until the sugar has melted.

Menus for Entertaining

When you have guests to feed, clever combining of well-chosen dishes can quickly result in an impressive menu in next to no time. The menu suggestions below feature main course vegetarian meals, quick and easy starters, salads and desserts, specially chosen for their ease of preparation and tastiness.

Menu 1

Warm focaccia bread with salt crystals and olives

Asparagus Rolls with Herb Butter Sauce

Lentil Stir-fry served with a green salad

Summer berries with Kirsch and vanilla sugar

Menu 2

Grilled cherry tomato and basil salad

Mushrooms with Leeks and Stilton

Potato, Broccoli and Red Pepper Stir-fry

Baked banana and orange segments

Menu 3

Poached asparagus with crème fraîche and lemon

Ciabatta Rolls with Courgettes and Saffron

Red Fried Rice

Warm ginger cake with golden syrup

Menu 4

French bread slices with tapenade and mozzarella

Lemon and Parmesan Cappellini with Herb Bread

Fresh Spinach and Avocado Salad

Banana and amaretti with passion fruit cream

Menu 5

Fresh tomato and coriander with poppadoms

Bengali-style Vegetables

Cumin-spiced Marrow and Spinach

Spiced potato and cauliflower Fresh fruit to follow

Menu 6

Crudités with mayonnaise dip

Potato, Spinach and Pine Nut Gratin

Vegetable Kebabs with Mustard and Honey

Grilled mascarpone plums

Melon and Basil Soup

A deliciously refreshing, chilled fruit soup, just right for a hot summer's day.

Serves 4–6

INGREDIENTS
2 Charentais or rock melons
75 g/3 oz/⅓ cup caster sugar
175 ml/6 fl oz/¾ cup water
finely grated rind and juice of 1 lime
45 ml/3 tbsp shredded fresh basil
fresh basil leaves, to garnish

basil

caster sugar

lime

Charentais melon

1 Cut the melons in half across the middle. Scrape out the seeds and discard. Using a melon baller, scoop out 20–24 balls and set aside for the garnish. Scoop out the remaining flesh and place in a blender or food processor.

2 Place the sugar, water and lime zest in a small pan over a low heat. Stir until dissolved, bring to the boil and simmer for 2–3 minutes. Remove from the heat and leave to cool slightly. Pour half the mixture into the blender or food processor with the melon flesh. Blend until smooth, adding the remaining syrup and lime juice to taste.

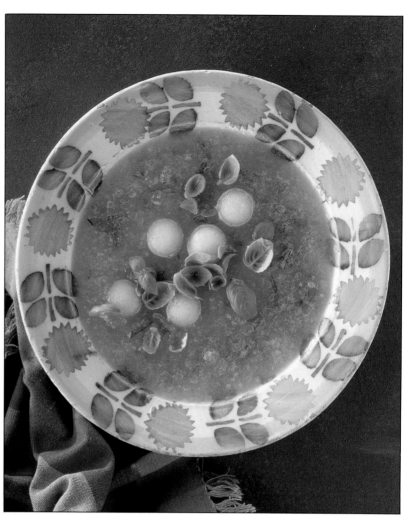

3 Pour the mixture into a bowl, stir in the basil and chill. Serve garnished with basil leaves and melon balls.

COOK'S TIP
Add the syrup in two stages, as the amount of sugar needed will depend on the sweetness of the melon.

Leek, Parsnip and Ginger Soup

A flavoursome winter warmer, with the added spiciness of fresh ginger.

Serves 4–6

INGREDIENTS

30 ml/2 tbsp olive oil
225 g/8 oz leeks, sliced
25 g/1 oz fresh ginger root, finely
   chopped
675 g/1½ lb parsnips, roughly
   chopped
300 ml/½ pint/1¼ cups dry white
   wine
1.1 litres/2 pints/5 cups vegetable
   stock or water
salt and freshly ground black pepper
low-fat fromage blanc, to garnish
paprika, to garnish

ginger

parsnips

vegetable stock

leek

1 Heat the oil in a large pan and add the leeks and ginger. Cook gently for 2–3 minutes, until the leeks start to soften.

2 Add the parsnips and cook for a further 7–8 minutes.

3 Pour in the wine and stock or water and bring to the boil. Reduce the heat and simmer for 20–30 minutes or until the parsnips are tender.

4 Purée in a blender until smooth. Season to taste. Reheat and garnish with a swirl of fromage blanc and a light dusting of paprika.

Chilled Fresh Tomato Soup

This effortless uncooked soup can be made in minutes.

Serves 4–6

INGREDIENTS

1.5 kg/3–3½ lb ripe tomatoes, peeled
   and roughly chopped
4 garlic cloves, crushed
30 ml/2 tbsp extra-virgin olive oil
   (optional)
30 ml/2 tbsp balsamic vinegar
freshly ground black pepper
4 slices wholemeal bread
low-fat fromage blanc, to garnish

wholemeal bread

garlic

fromage blanc

peppercorns

tomato

COOK'S TIP

For the best flavour, it is important to use only fully ripened, flavourful tomatoes in this soup.

1 Place the tomatoes in a blender with the garlic and olive oil if using. Blend until smooth.

2 Pass the mixture through a sieve to remove the seeds. Stir in the balsamic vinegar and season to taste with pepper. Leave in the fridge to chill.

3 Toast the bread lightly on both sides. Whilst still hot, cut off the crusts and slice in half horizontally. Place the toast on a board with the uncooked sides facing down and, using a circular motion, rub to remove any doughy pieces of bread.

4 Cut each slice into 4 triangles. Place on a grill pan and toast the uncooked sides until lightly golden. Garnish each bowl of soup with a spoonful of fromage blanc and serve with the melba toast.

Broccoli and Almond Soup

The creaminess of the toasted almonds combines perfectly with the slight bitterness of the taste of broccoli.

Serves 4–6

INGREDIENTS
50 g/2 oz/²⁄₃ cup ground almonds
675 g/1½ lb broccoli
850 ml/1½ pints/3¾ cups vegetable stock or water
300 ml/½ pint/1¼ cups skimmed milk
salt and freshly ground black pepper

ground almonds

skimmed milk

broccoli

1 Preheat the oven to 180°C/350°F/ Gas 4. Spread the ground almonds evenly on a baking sheet and toast in the oven for about 10 minutes, or until golden. Reserve ¼ of the almonds and set aside for the garnish.

2 Cut the broccoli into small florets and steam for 6–7 minutes or until tender.

3 Place the remaining toasted almonds, broccoli, stock or water and milk in a blender and blend until smooth. Season to taste.

4 Reheat the soup and serve sprinkled with the reserved toasted almonds.

Red Onion and Beetroot Soup

This beautiful vivid ruby-red soup will look stunning at any dinner party.

Serves 4–6

INGREDIENTS
15 ml/1 tbsp olive oil
350 g/12 oz red onions, sliced
2 garlic cloves, crushed
275 g/10 oz cooked beetroot, cut into sticks
1.1 litres/2 pints/5 cups vegetable stock or water
50 g/2 oz/1 cup cooked soup pasta
30 ml/2 tbsp raspberry vinegar
salt and freshly ground black pepper
low-fat yogurt or fromage blanc, to garnish
snipped chives, to garnish

garlic

red onion

beetroot

pasta

chives

1 Heat the olive oil and add the onions and garlic.

2 Cook gently for about 20 minutes or until soft and tender.

3 Add the beetroot, stock or water, cooked pasta shapes and vinegar and heat through. Season to taste.

4 Ladle into bowls. Top each one with a spoonful of yogurt or fromage blanc and sprinkle with chives.

COOK'S TIP

Try substituting cooked barley for the pasta to give extra nuttiness.

Cauliflower, Flageolet and Fennel Seed Soup

The sweet, anise-liquorice flavour of the fennel seeds gives a delicious edge to this hearty soup.

Serves 4–6

INGREDIENTS
15 ml/1 tbsp olive oil
1 garlic clove, crushed
1 onion, chopped
10 ml/2 tsp fennel seeds
1 cauliflower, cut into small florets
2 × 400 g/14 oz cans flageolet beans, drained and rinsed
1.1 litres/2 pints/5 cups vegetable stock or water
salt and freshly ground black pepper
chopped fresh parsley, to garnish
toasted slices of French bread, to serve

flageolet beans

French bread

onion

garlic

cauliflower

fennel seeds

parsley

1 Heat the olive oil. Add the garlic, onion and fennel seeds and cook gently for 5 minutes or until softened.

2 Add the cauliflower, half of the beans and the stock or water.

3 Bring to the boil. Reduce the heat and simmer for 10 minutes or until the cauliflower is tender.

4 Pour the soup into a blender and blend until smooth. Stir in the remaining beans and season to taste. Reheat and pour into bowls. Sprinkle with chopped parsley and serve with toasted slices of French bread.

Cucumber and Alfalfa Tortillas

Wheat tortillas are extremely simple to prepare at home. Served with a crisp, fresh salsa, they make a marvellous light lunch or supper dish.

Serves 4

INGREDIENTS
225 g/8 oz/2 cups plain flour
pinch of salt
45 ml/3 tbsp olive oil
100 ml–150 ml/4–5 fl oz/½–⅔ cup
   warm water
lime wedges, to garnish

FOR THE SALSA
1 red onion, finely chopped
1 fresh red chilli, seeded and finely
   chopped
30 ml/2 tbsp chopped fresh dill or
   coriander
½ cucumber, peeled and chopped
175 g/6 oz alfalfa sprouts

FOR THE SAUCE
1 large avocado, peeled and stoned
juice of 1 lime
25 g/1 oz/2 tbsp soft goat's cheese
pinch of paprika

avocado

goat's cheese

red chilli

cucumber

dill   alfalfa sprouts

COOK'S TIP

When peeling the avocado be sure to scrape off the bright green flesh from immediately under the skin as this gives the sauce its vivid green colour.

1 Mix all the salsa ingredients together in a bowl and set aside.

2 To make the sauce, place the avocado, lime juice and goat's cheese in a food processor or blender and blend until smooth. Place in a bowl and cover with clear film. Dust with paprika just before serving.

3 To make the tortillas, place the flour and salt in a food processor, add the oil and blend. Gradually add the water (the amount will vary depending on the type of flour). Stop adding water when a stiff dough has formed. Turn out onto a floured board and knead until smooth. Cover with a damp cloth.

4 Divide the mixture into 8 pieces. Knead each piece for a couple of minutes and form into a ball. Flatten and roll out each ball to a 23 cm/9 in circle.

5 Heat an ungreased heavy-based pan. Cook 1 tortilla at a time for about 30 seconds on each side. Place the cooked tortillas in a clean tea-towel and repeat until you have 8 tortillas.

6 To serve, spread each tortilla with a spoonful of avocado sauce, top with salsa and roll up. Garnish with lime wedges.

Baked Herb Crêpes

These mouth-watering, light herb crêpes make a striking starter at a dinner party, but are equally splendid served with a crisp salad for lunch.

Serves 4

INGREDIENTS
25 g/1 oz chopped fresh herbs
  (e.g. parsley, thyme, and chervil)
15 ml/1 tbsp sunflower oil, plus extra
  for frying
100 ml/4 fl oz/½ cup skimmed milk
3 × size 3 eggs
25 g/1 oz/¼ cup plain flour
pinch of salt

FOR THE SAUCE
30 ml/2 tbsp olive oil
1 small onion, chopped
2 garlic cloves, crushed
15 ml/1 tbsp grated fresh ginger root
1 × 400 g/14 oz can chopped
  tomatoes

FOR THE FILLING
450 g/1 lb fresh spinach
175 g/6 oz/¾ cup ricotta cheese
25 g/1 oz/2 tbsp pine nuts, toasted
5 halves sun-dried tomatoes in olive
  oil, drained and chopped
30 ml/2 tbsp shredded fresh basil
salt, nutmeg and freshly ground black
  pepper
4 egg whites

onion

parsley

ginger

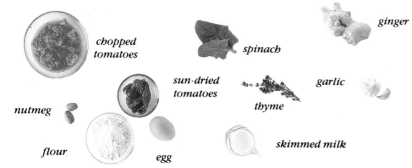

chopped
tomatoes

sun-dried
tomatoes

garlic

spinach

thyme

nutmeg

flour

egg

skimmed milk

1 To make the crêpes, place the herbs and oil in a blender and blend until smooth, pushing down any whole pieces with a spatula. Add the milk, eggs, flour and salt and process again until smooth and pale green. Leave to rest for 30 minutes.

2 Heat a small non-stick crêpe or frying pan and add a very small amount of oil. Pour out any excess oil and pour in a ladleful of the batter. Swirl around to cover the base. Cook for 1–2 minutes, turn over and cook the other side. Repeat to make 8 crêpes.

3 To make the sauce, heat the oil in a small pan. Add the onion, garlic and ginger and cook gently for 5 minutes until softened. Add the tomatoes and cook for a further 10–15 minutes until the mixture thickens. Purée, sieve and set aside.

4 To make the filling, wash the spinach, removing any large stalks, and place in a large pan with only the water that clings to the leaves. Cover and cook, stirring once, until the spinach has just wilted. Remove from the heat and refresh in cold water. Place in a sieve or colander, squeeze out the excess water and chop finely. Mix the spinach with the ricotta, pine nuts, sun-dried tomatoes and basil. Season with salt, nutmeg and freshly ground black pepper.

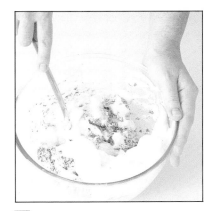

5 Preheat the oven to 190°C/375°F/ Gas 5. Whisk the 4 egg whites until stiff but not dry. Fold ⅓ into the spinach and ricotta to lighten the mixture, then gently fold in the rest.

6 Taking each crêpe at a time, place on a lightly oiled baking sheet. Place a large spoonful of filling on each one and fold into quarters. Repeat until all the filling and crêpes are used up. Bake in the oven for 10–15 minutes or until set. Reheat the tomato sauce to serve with the crêpes.

COOK'S TIP

If preferred, use plain sun-dried tomatoes without any oil, and soak them in warm water for 20 minutes before using.

Buckwheat Blinis

These delectable light pancakes originated in Russia.
For a special occasion, serve with a small glass of
chilled vodka.

Serves 4

INGREDIENTS
5 ml/1 tsp easy-blend dry yeast
250 ml/8 fl oz/1 cup skimmed milk,
  warmed
40 g/1½ oz/⅓ cup buckwheat flour
40 g/1½ oz/⅓ cup plain flour
10ml/2 tsp caster sugar
pinch of salt
1 × size 3 egg, separated
oil, for frying

FOR THE AVOCADO CREAM
1 large avocado
75 g/3 oz/⅓ cup low-fat fromage
  blanc
juice of 1 lime

FOR THE PICKLED BEETROOT
225 g/8 oz beetroot
45 ml/3 tbsp lime juice
snipped chives, to garnish
cracked black peppercorns, to garnish

beetroot
egg   *avocado*
          buckwheat flour
lime
          chives
*fromage
blanc*
     skimmed milk

1 Mix the dry yeast with the milk, then
mix with the next 4 ingredients and the
egg yolk. Cover with a cloth and leave to
prove for about 40 minutes. Whisk the
egg white until stiff but not dry and fold
into the blini mixture.

2 Heat a little oil in a non-stick pan and
add a ladleful of batter to make a 10 cm/
4 in pancake. Cook for 2–3 minutes on
each side. Repeat with the remaining
batter mixture to make 8 blinis.

3 Cut the avocado in half and remove
the stone. Peel and place the flesh in a
blender with the fromage blanc and lime
juice. Blend until smooth.

4 Peel the beetroot and shred finely.
Mix with the lime juice. To serve, top
each blini with a spoonful of avocado
cream. Serve with the pickled beetroot
and garnish with snipped chives and
cracked black peppercorns.

Cheese-stuffed Pears

These pears, with their scrumptious creamy topping, make a sublime dish when served with a simple salad.

Serves 4

INGREDIENTS

50 g/2 oz/¼ cup ricotta cheese
50 g/2 oz/¼ cup dolcelatte cheese
15 ml/1 tbsp honey
½ celery stick, finely sliced
8 green olives, pitted and roughly
  chopped
4 dates, stoned and cut into thin strips
pinch of paprika
4 ripe pears
150 ml/¼ pint/⅔ cup apple juice

honey

pear

apple juice

dates

dolcelatte

celery

olives

COOK'S TIP

Choose ripe pears in season such as Conference, William or Comice.

1 Preheat the oven to 200°C/400°F/ Gas 6. Place the ricotta in a bowl and crumble in the dolcelatte. Add the rest of the ingredients except for the pears and apple juice and mix well.

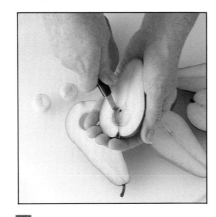

2 Halve the pears lengthwise and use a melon baller to remove the cores. Place in a ovenproof dish and divide the filling equally between them.

3 Pour in the apple juice and cover the dish with foil. Bake for 20 minutes or until the pears are tender.

4 Remove the foil and place the dish under a hot grill for 3 minutes. Serve immediately.

Soufflé Omelette

This delectable soufflé omlette is light and delicate enough to melt in the mouth.

Serves 1

INGREDIENTS
2 eggs, separated
30 ml/2 tbsp cold water
15 ml/1 tbsp chopped fresh coriander
salt and freshly ground black pepper
7.5 ml/½ tbsp olive oil
30 ml/2 tbsp mango chutney
25 g/1 oz/¼ cup Jarlsberg cheese, grated

Jarlsberg

mango chutney

eggs

coriander

COOK'S TIP

A light hand is essential to the success of this dish. Do not overmix the egg whites into the yolks or the mixture will be heavy.

1 Beat the egg yolks together with the cold water, coriander and seasoning.

2 Whisk the egg whites until stiff but not dry and gently fold into the egg yolk mixture.

3 Heat the oil in a frying pan, pour in the egg mixture and reduce the heat. Do not stir. Cook until the omelette becomes puffy and golden brown on the underside (carefully lift one edge with a palette knife to check).

4 Spoon on the chutney and sprinkle on the Jarlsberg. Fold over and slide onto a warm plate. Eat immediately. (If preferred, before adding the chutney and cheese, place the pan under a hot grill to set the top.)

Nutty Cheese Balls

An extremely quick and simple recipe. Try making a smaller version to serve as canapés at a drinks party.

Serves 4

INGREDIENTS
225 g/8 oz/1 cup low-fat soft cheese
   such as Quark
50 g/2 oz/¼ cup dolcelatte cheese
15 ml/1 tbsp finely chopped onion
15 ml/1 tbsp finely chopped celery
   stick
15 ml/1 tbsp finely chopped parsley
15 ml/1 tbsp finely chopped gherkin
5 ml/1 tsp brandy or port (optional)
pinch of paprika
50 g/2 oz/½ cup walnuts, roughly
   chopped
90 ml/6 tbsp snipped chives
salt and freshly ground black pepper

dolcelatte

celery

gherkins

soft cheese

onion

walnuts

chives

parsley

paprika

1 Beat the soft cheese and dolcelatte together using a spoon.

2 Mix in all the remaining ingredients, except the snipped chives.

3 Divide the mixture into 12 pieces and roll into balls.

4 Roll each ball gently in the snipped chives. Leave in the fridge to chill for about an hour before serving.

Sweet Potato Roulade

Sweet potato works particularly well as the base for this roulade. Serve in thin slices for a truly impressive dinner party dish.

Serves 6

INGREDIENTS

225 g/8 oz/1 cup low-fat soft cheese such as Quark
75 ml/5 tbsp low-fat yogurt
6–8 spring onions, finely sliced
30 ml/2 tbsp chopped brazil nuts, roasted
450 g/1 lb sweet potatoes, peeled and cubed
12 allspice berries, crushed
4 eggs, separated
50 g/2 oz/¼ cup Edam cheese, finely grated
salt and freshly ground black pepper
15 ml/1 tbsp sesame seeds

soft cheese

sesame seeds

sweet potato

yogurt

Edam

brazil nuts

spring onions

peppercorns

egg

1 Preheat the oven to 200°C/400°F/ Gas 6. Grease and line a 33 × 25 cm/ 13 × 10 in Swiss roll tin with non-stick baking paper, snipping the corners with scissors to fit.

2 In a small bowl, mix together the soft cheese, yogurt, spring onions and brazil nuts. Set aside.

3 Boil or steam the sweet potato until tender. Drain well. Place in a food processor with the allspice and blend until smooth. Spoon into a bowl and stir in the egg yolks and Edam. Season to taste.

4 Whisk the egg whites until stiff but not dry. Fold ⅓ of the egg whites into the sweet potatoes to lighten the mixture before gently folding in the rest.

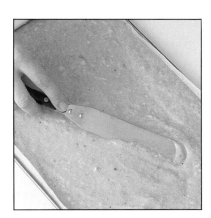

5 Pour into the prepared tin, tipping it to get the mixture right into the corners. Smooth gently with a palette knife and cook in the oven for 10–15 minutes.

COOK'S TIP

Choose the orange-fleshed variety of sweet potato for the most striking colour.

6 Meanwhile, lay a large sheet of greaseproof paper on a clean tea-towel and sprinkle with the sesame seeds. When the roulade is cooked, tip it onto the paper, trim the edges and roll it up. Leave to cool. When cool carefully unroll, spread with the filling and roll up again. Cut into slices to serve.

Ratatouille with Soft Cheese Croûtons

Crisp croûtons and creamy Camembert provide a tasty topping on hot ratatouille. Choose a quality brand of ratatouille or make your own.

Serves 2

INGREDIENTS
3 thick slices of white bread
225 g/8 oz firm Camembert cheese
60 ml/4 tbsp olive oil
1 garlic clove, chopped
400 g/14 oz can ratatouille
parsley sprigs, to garnish

ratatouille

parsley

garlic clove

white bread

Camembert cheese

1 Trim the crusts from the bread slices and discard. Cut the bread into 2.5 cm/ 1 in squares. Cut the Camembert into 2.5 cm/1 in cubes.

2 Heat 45 ml/3 tbsp of the oil in a frying pan. Add the bread and cook over a high heat for 5 minutes, stirring constantly, until golden all over. Reduce the heat, add the garlic and cook for 1 minute more. Remove the croûtons with a slotted spoon.

3 Tip the ratatouille into a pan and place over a medium heat, stirring occasionally, until hot.

4 Heat the remaining oil in the frying pan. Add the cheese cubes and sear over a high heat for 1 minute. Divide the hot ratatouille between two serving bowls, spoon the croûtons and cheese on top, garnish with the parsley and serve at once.

Omelette aux Fines Herbs

Eggs respond well to fast cooking and combine beautifully with a handful of fresh herbs. Serve with oven-ready chips and a green salad.

Serves 1

INGREDIENTS
3 eggs
30 ml/2 tbsp chopped fresh parsley
30 ml/2 tbsp chopped fresh chervil
30 ml/2 tbsp chopped fresh tarragon
15 ml/1 tbsp chopped fresh chives
15 ml/½ oz/1 tbsp butter
salt and freshly ground black pepper
350 g/12 oz oven-ready chips,
   to serve
115 g/4 oz green salad, to serve
1 tomato, to serve

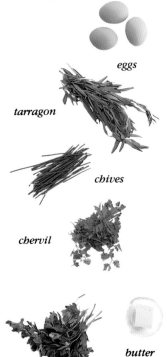

eggs

tarragon

chives

chervil

butter

parsley

1 Break the eggs into a bowl, season to taste and beat with a fork, then add the chopped herbs.

2 Heat an omelette or frying pan over a fierce heat, add the butter and cook until it foams and browns. Quickly pour in the beaten egg and stir briskly with the back of the fork. When the egg is two-thirds scrambled, let the omelette finish cooking for 10–15 seconds more.

3 Tap the handle of the omelette or frying pan sharply with your fist to make the omelette jump up the sides of the pan, fold and turn onto a plate. Serve with oven-ready chips, green salad and a halved tomato.

COOK'S TIP

From start to finish, an omelette should be cooked and on the table in less than a minute. For best results use free-range eggs at room temperature.

Cheese en Croûte with Tomato Sauce

Melt-in-the-mouth cheese sandwiches, pan-fried and served with a tomato sauce.

Serves 4

INGREDIENTS
50 g/2 oz/¼ cup butter, softened
1 small onion, chopped
400 g/14 oz can chopped tomatoes
large thyme sprig
8 slices of white bread
115 g/4 oz mature Cheddar cheese
2 eggs
30 ml/2 tbsp milk
30 ml/2 tbsp groundnut oil
salt and freshly ground black pepper
8 cos lettuce leaves, to serve

thyme

eggs

chopped tomatoes

onion

milk

Cheddar cheese

butter

white bread

1 Melt 25 g/1 oz/2 tbsp of the butter in a frying pan. Add the onion and cook for 3–4 minutes until soft.

2 Stir in the chopped tomatoes. Strip the leaves from the thyme sprig and stir them into the pan. Add salt and pepper to taste, then cover the pan and cook for 5 minutes.

3 Meanwhile, spread the remaining butter over the slices of bread.

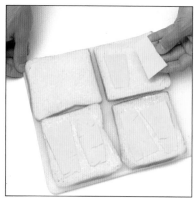

4 Slice the cheese thinly. Arrange on 4 slices of bread and sandwich with the remaining slices. Trim the crusts.

5 Beat the eggs and milk together in a bowl. Add salt and pepper to taste and pour into a shallow dish.

6 Heat the oil in a large frying pan. Dip each sandwich in the egg mixture until well-coated. Add to the hot oil and fry for 2 minutes on each side, until the coating is golden and the cheese has melted. Cut each sandwich into quarters. Arrange on individual plates garnished with the cos lettuce leaves. Serve the tomato sauce in a bowl to one side.

COOK'S TIP
If the tomato sauce is a little tart, add a pinch of sugar, or liven it up with a dash of Tabasco.

Sesame Noodle Salad with Hot Peanuts

An orient-inspired salad with crunchy vegetables and a light soy dressing. The hot peanuts make a surprisingly successful union with the cold noodles.

Serves 4

INGREDIENTS

350 g/12 oz egg noodles
2 carrots, peeled and cut into fine
  julienne strips
½ cucumber, peeled and cut into
  1 cm/½ in cubes
115 g/4 oz celeriac, peeled and cut
  into fine julienne strips
6 spring onions, finely sliced
8 canned water chestnuts, drained
  and finely sliced
175 g/6 oz beansprouts
1 small fresh green chilli, seeded and
  finely chopped
30 ml/2 tbsp sesame seeds, to serve
115 g/4 oz/1 cup peanuts, to serve

FOR THE DRESSING

15 ml/1 tbsp dark soy sauce
15 ml/1 tbsp light soy sauce
15 ml/1 tbsp runny honey
15 ml/1 tbsp rice wine or dry sherry
15 ml/1 tbsp sesame oil

2 Drain the noodles, refresh in cold water, then drain again.

3 Mix the noodles with all of the prepared vegetables.

1 Preheat the oven to 200°C/400°F/ Gas 6. Cook the egg noodles in boiling water, following the instructions on the side of the packet.

celeriac

beansprouts

green chili

water chestnuts

cucumber

carrot

peanuts

sesame seeds

spring onion

noodles

4 Combine the dressing ingredients in a small bowl, then toss into the noodle and vegetable mixture. Divide the salad between 4 plates.

5 Place the sesame seeds and peanuts on separate baking trays and place in the oven. Take the sesame seeds out after 5 minutes and continue to cook the peanuts for a further 5 minutes until evenly browned.

6 Sprinkle the sesame seeds and peanuts evenly over each portion and serve at once.

Penne with Aubergine and Mint Pesto

This splendid variation on the classic Italian pesto uses fresh mint rather than basil for a different flavour.

Serves 4

INGREDIENTS
2 large aubergines
salt
450 g/1 lb penne
50 g/2 oz walnut halves

FOR THE PESTO
25 g/1 oz fresh mint
15 g/½ oz flat-leaf parsley
40 g/1½ oz walnuts
40 g/1½ oz Parmesan cheese, finely grated
2 garlic cloves
90 ml/6 tbsp olive oil
salt and freshly ground black pepper

penne

garlic

walnuts

aubergine

olive oil

parsley

mint

Parmesan

1 Cut the aubergines lengthwise into 1 cm/½ in slices.

2 Cut the slices again crossways to give short strips.

3 Layer the strips in a colander with salt and leave to stand for 30 minutes over a plate to catch any juices. Rinse well in cool water and drain.

4 Place all the pesto ingredients, except the oil in a blender or food processor, blend until smooth, then gradually add the oil in a thin stream until the mixture amalgamates. Season to taste.

5 Cook the penne following the instructions on the side of the packet for about 8 minutes or until nearly cooked. Add the aubergine and cook for a further 3 minutes.

6 Drain well and mix in the mint pesto and walnut halves. Serve immediately.

Campanelle with Yellow Pepper Sauce

Roasted yellow peppers make a deliciously sweet and creamy sauce to serve with pasta.

Serves 4

INGREDIENTS
2 yellow peppers
50 g/2 oz/¼ cup soft goat's cheese
115 g/4 oz/½ cup low-fat fromage blanc
salt and freshly ground black pepper
450 g/1 lb short pasta such as campanelle or fusilli
50 g/2 oz/¼ cup flaked almonds, toasted, to serve

pepper

fromage blanc

flaked almonds

goat's cheese

campanelle

1 Place the whole yellow peppers under a preheated grill until charred and blistered. Place in a plastic bag to cool. Peel and remove the seeds.

2 Place the pepper flesh in a blender with the goat's cheese and fromage blanc. Blend until smooth. Season with salt and lots of black pepper.

3 Cook the pasta following the instructions on the side of the packet until *al dente*. Drain well.

4 Toss with the sauce and serve sprinkled with the toasted flaked almonds.

Spaghetti with Black Olive and Mushroom Sauce

A rich pungent sauce topped with sweet cherry tomatoes.

Serves 4

INGREDIENTS

15 ml/1 tbsp olive oil
1 garlic clove, chopped
225 g/8 oz mushrooms, chopped
150 g/5 oz/generous ½ cup black
   olives, pitted
30 ml/2 tbsp chopped fresh parsley
1 fresh red chilli, seeded and chopped
450 g/1 lb spaghetti
225 g/8 oz cherry tomatoes
slivers of Parmesan cheese, to serve
   (optional)

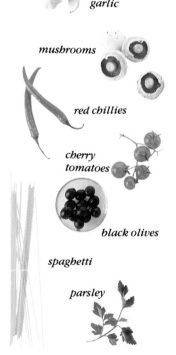

garlic

mushrooms

red chillies

cherry
tomatoes

black olives

spaghetti

parsley

1 Heat the oil in a large pan. Add the garlic and cook for 1 minute. Add the mushrooms, cover, and cook over a medium heat for 5 minutes.

2 Place the mushrooms in a blender or food processor with the olives, parsley and red chilli. Blend until smooth.

3 Cook the pasta following the instructions on the side of the packet until *al dente*. Drain well and return to the pan. Add the olive mixture and toss together until the pasta is well coated. Cover and keep warm.

4 Heat an ungreased frying pan and shake the cherry tomatoes around until they start to split (about 2–3 minutes). Serve the pasta topped with the tomatoes and garnished with slivers of Parmesan, if liked.

Tagliatelle with Pea Sauce, Asparagus and Broad Beans

A creamy pea sauce makes a wonderful combination with the crunchy young vegetables.

Serves 4

INGREDIENTS
15 ml/1 tbsp olive oil
1 garlic clove, crushed
6 spring onions, sliced
225 g/8 oz/1 cup frozen peas,
  defrosted
350 g/12 oz fresh young asparagus
30 ml/2 tbsp chopped fresh sage, plus
extra leaves to garnish
finely grated rind of 2 lemons
450 ml/¾ pint/1¾ cups vegetable
  stock or water
225 g/8 oz frozen broad beans,
  defrosted
450 g/1 lb tagliatelle
60 ml/4 tbsp low-fat yogurt

lemon

garlic

asparagus

broad beans

peas

yogurt

tagliatelle

sage

spring onion

1 Heat the oil in a pan. Add the garlic and spring onions and cook gently for 2–3 minutes until softened.

2 Add the peas and ⅓ of the asparagus, together with the sage, lemon rind and stock or water. Bring to the boil, reduce the heat and simmer for 10 minutes until tender. Purée in a blender until smooth.

3 Meanwhile remove the outer skins from the broad beans and discard.

4 Cut the remaining asparagus into 5 cm/2 in lengths trimming off any tough fibrous stems, and blanch in boiling water for 2 minutes.

5 Cook the tagliatelle following the instructions on the side of the packet until *al dente*. Drain well.

COOK'S TIP

Frozen peas and beans have been used here to cut down the preparation time, but the dish tastes even better if you use fresh young vegetables when in season.

6 Add the cooked asparagus and shelled beans to the sauce and reheat. Stir in the yogurt and toss into the tagliatelle. Garnish with a few extra sage leaves and serve.

Coriander Ravioli with Pumpkin Filling

A stunning herb pasta with a superb creamy pumpkin and roast garlic filling.

Serves 4–6

INGREDIENTS

200 g/7 oz/scant 1 cup strong
   unbleached white flour
2 eggs
pinch of salt
45 ml/3 tbsp chopped fresh coriander
coriander sprigs, to garnish

FOR THE FILLING

4 garlic cloves in their skins
450 g/1 lb pumpkin, peeled and seeds
   removed
115 g/4 oz/½ cup ricotta
4 halves sun-dried tomatoes in olive
   oil, drained and finely chopped, but
   reserve 30 ml/2 tbsp of the oil
freshly ground black pepper

coriander

pumpkin

egg

garlic

flour

ricotta

sun-dried tomatoes

1 Place the flour, eggs, salt and coriander into a food processor. Pulse until combined.

2 Place the dough on a lightly floured board and knead well for 5 minutes, until smooth. Wrap in clear film and leave to rest in the fridge for 20 minutes.

3 Preheat the oven to 200°C/400°F/ Gas 6. Place the garlic cloves on a baking sheet and bake for 10 minutes until softened. Steam the pumpkin for 5–8 minutes until tender and drain well. Peel the garlic cloves and mash into the pumpkin together with the ricotta and drained sun-dried tomatoes. Season with black pepper.

4 Divide the pasta into 4 pieces and flatten slightly. Using a pasta machine, on its thinnest setting, roll out each piece. Leave the sheets of pasta on a clean tea-towel until slightly dried.

5 Using a 7.5 cm/3 in crinkle-edged round cutter, stamp out 36 rounds.

6 Top 18 of the rounds with a teaspoonful of mixture, brush the edges with water and place another round of pasta on top. Press firmly around the edges to seal. Bring a large pan of water to the boil, add the ravioli and cook for 3–4 minutes. Drain well and toss into the reserved tomato oil. Serve garnished with coriander sprigs.

Capellini with Rocket, Mange-tout and Pine Nuts

A light but filling pasta dish with the added pepperiness of fresh rocket.

Serves 4

INGREDIENTS
250 g/9 oz capellini or angel-hair pasta
225 g/8 oz mange-tout
175 g/6 oz rocket
50 g/2 oz/¼ cup pine nuts, roasted
30 ml/2 tbsp Parmesan cheese, finely grated (optional)
30 ml/2 tbsp olive oil (optional)

rocket

Parmesan

pine nuts

capellini

mange-tout

1 Cook the capellini or angel-hair pasta following the instructions on the side of the packet until *al dente*.

2 Meanwhile, carefully top and tail the mange-tout.

3 As soon as the pasta is cooked, drop in the rocket and mange-tout. Drain immediately.

4 Toss the pasta with the roasted pine nuts, and Parmesan and olive oil if using. Serve at once.

COOK'S TIP
Olive oil and Parmesan are optional as they obviously raise the fat content.

Pasta Bows with Fennel and Walnut Sauce

A scrumptious blend of walnuts and crisp steamed fennel.

Serves 4

INGREDIENTS
75 g/3 oz/½ cup walnuts, roughly
    chopped
1 garlic clove
25 g/1 oz fresh flat-leaf parsley, picked
    from the stalks
115 g/4 oz/½ cup ricotta cheese
450 g/1 lb pasta bows
450 g/1 lb fennel bulbs
chopped walnuts, to garnish

garlic

pasta bows

ricotta

fennel

parsley

walnut halves

chopped walnuts

1 Place the chopped walnuts, garlic and parsley in a food processor. Pulse until roughly chopped. Transfer to a bowl and stir in the ricotta.

2 Cook the pasta following the instructions on the side of the packet until *al dente*. Drain well.

3 Slice the fennel thinly and steam for 4–5 minutes until just tender but still crisp.

4 Return the pasta to the pan and add the walnut mixture and the fennel. Toss well and sprinkle with the chopped walnuts. Serve immediately.

Double Tomato Tagliatelle

Sun-dried tomatoes add pungency to this dish, while the grilled fresh tomatoes add bite.

Serves 4

INGREDIENTS
45 ml/3 tbsp olive oil
1 garlic clove, crushed
1 small onion, chopped
50 ml/2 fl oz/¼ cup dry white wine
6 sun-dried tomatoes, chopped
30 ml/2 tbsp chopped fresh parsley
50 g/2 oz/½ cup stoned black
  olives, halved
450 g/1 lb fresh tagliatelle
4 tomatoes, halved
Parmesan cheese, to serve
salt and freshly ground black pepper

tomatoes
parsley
garlic clove
sun-dried tomatoes
tagliatelle
dry white wine
onion
black olives
Parmesan cheese

COOK'S TIP
It is essential to buy Parmesan in a piece for this dish. Find a good source – fresh Parmesan should not be unacceptably hard – and shave or grate it yourself. The flavour will be much more intense than that of the ready-grated product.

1 Heat 30 ml/2 tbsp of the oil in a pan. Add the garlic and onion and cook for 2–3 minutes, stirring occasionally. Add the wine, sun-dried tomatoes and the parsley. Cook for 2 minutes. Stir in the black olives.

2 Bring a large pan of salted water to the boil. Add the fresh tagliatelle and cook for 2–3 minutes until just tender. Preheat the grill.

3 Put the tomatoes on a tray and brush with the remaining oil. Grill for 3–4 minutes.

4 Drain the pasta, return it to the pan and toss with the sauce. Serve with the grilled tomatoes, freshly ground black pepper and shavings of Parmesan.

Penne with Fennel Concassé and Blue Cheese

The aniseed flavour of the fennel makes it the perfect partner for tomato, especially when topped with blue cheese.

Serves 2

INGREDIENTS
1 fennel bulb
225 g/8 oz penne or other dried
  pasta shapes
30 ml/2 tbsp extra virgin olive oil
1 shallot, finely chopped
300 ml/½ pint/1¼ cups passata
pinch of sugar
5 ml/1 tsp chopped fresh oregano
115 g/4 oz blue cheese
salt and freshly ground black pepper

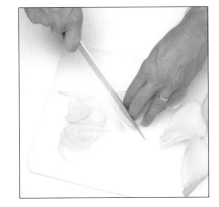

oregano

shallot

fennel bulb

penne

passata

sugar

blue cheese

1 Cut the fennel bulb in half. Cut away the hard core and root. Slice the fennel thinly, then cut the slices into strips.

2 Bring a large pan of salted water to the boil. Add the pasta and cook for 10–12 minutes until just tender.

3 Meanwhile, heat the oil in a small saucepan. Add the fennel and shallot and cook for 2–3 minutes over a high heat, stirring occasionally.

4 Add the passata, sugar and oregano. Cover the pan and simmer gently for 10–12 minutes, until the fennel is tender. Add salt and pepper to taste. Drain the pasta and return it to the pan and toss with the sauce. Serve in bowls, with the blue cheese crumbled over the top.

Lemon and Parmesan Capellini with Herb Bread

Cream is thickened with Parmesan and flavoured with lemon to make a superb sauce for pasta.

Serves 2

INGREDIENTS

¹/₂ Granary baguette
50 g/2 oz/¹/₄ cup butter, softened
1 garlic clove, crushed
30 ml/2 tbsp chopped fresh herbs
225 g/8 oz dried or fresh capellini
250 ml/8 fl oz/1 cup single cream
75 g/3 oz Parmesan cheese, grated
finely grated rind of 1 lemon
salt and freshly ground black pepper

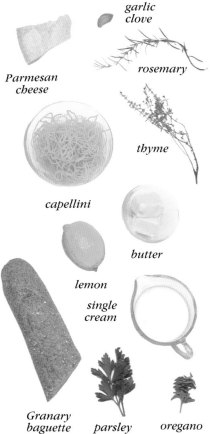

garlic clove

Parmesan cheese

rosemary

thyme

capellini

butter

lemon

single cream

Granary baguette   *parsley*   *oregano*

1 Preheat the oven to 200°C/400°F/ Gas 6. Cut the baguette into thick slices.

2 Put the butter in a bowl and beat with the garlic and herbs. Spread thickly over each slice of bread.

3 Reassemble the baguette. Wrap in foil, support on a baking sheet and bake for 10 minutes.

4 Meanwhile, bring a large pan of water to the boil and cook the pasta until just tender. Dried pasta will take 10–12 minutes; fresh pasta will be ready in 2–3 minutes.

5 Pour the cream into another pan and bring to the boil. Stir in the Parmesan and lemon rind. The sauce should thicken in about 30 seconds.

6 Drain the pasta, return it to the pan and toss with the sauce. Season to taste and sprinkle with a little chopped fresh parsley and grated lemon rind, if liked. Serve with the hot herb bread.

Summer Pasta Salad

Tender young vegetables in a light dressing make a delicious lunch.

Serves 2–3

INGREDIENTS

225 g/8 oz fusilli or other dried
 pasta shapes
115 g/4 oz baby carrots, trimmed
 and halved
115 g/4 oz baby sweetcorn, halved
 lengthways
50 g/2 oz mange-touts
115 g/4 oz young asparagus
 spears, trimmed
4 spring onions, trimmed
 and shredded
10 ml/2 tsp white wine vinegar
60 ml/4 tbsp extra virgin olive oil
15 ml/1 tbsp wholegrain mustard
salt and freshly ground black pepper

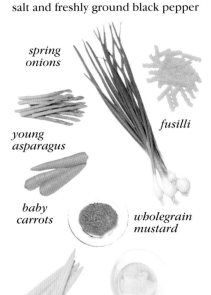

spring onions

fusilli

young asparagus

baby carrots

wholegrain mustard

baby sweetcorn

white wine vinegar

mange-touts

1 Bring a large pan of salted water to the boil. Add the pasta and cook for 10–12 minutes, until just tender. Meanwhile, cook the carrots and sweetcorn in a second pan of boiling salted water for 5 minutes.

2 Add the mange-touts and asparagus to the carrot mixture and cook for 2–3 minutes more. Drain all the vegetables and refresh under cold running water. Drain again.

3 Tip the vegetable mixture into a mixing bowl, add the spring onions and toss well together.

4 Drain the pasta, refresh it under cold running water and drain again. Toss with the vegetables. Mix the vinegar, olive oil and mustard in a jar. Add salt and pepper to taste, close the jar tightly and shake well. Pour the dressing over the salad. Toss well and serve.

Five-spice Vegetable Noodles

Vary this vegetable stir-fry by substituting mushrooms, bamboo shoots, beansprouts, mange-touts or water chestnuts for some or all of the vegetables suggested below.

Serves 2–3

INGREDIENTS
225 g/8 oz dried egg noodles
30 ml/2 tbsp sesame oil
2 carrots
1 celery stick
1 small fennel bulb
2 courgettes, halved and sliced
1 red chilli, seeded and chopped
2.5 cm/1 in piece of fresh root
  ginger, peeled and grated
1 garlic clove, crushed
7.5 ml/1½ tsp Chinese five-spice
  powder
2.5 ml/½ tsp ground cinnamon
4 spring onions, sliced
50 ml/2 fl oz/¼ cup warm water

1 Bring a large pan of salted water to the boil. Add the noodles and cook for 2–3 minutes until just tender. Drain the noodles, return them to the pan and toss in a little of the oil. Set aside.

carrots
celery stick
garlic clove
fennel bulb
egg noodles
courgettes
five-spice powder
spring onions
cinnamon
root ginger

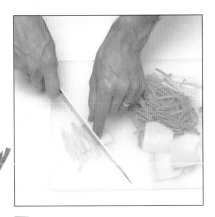

2 Cut the carrot and celery into julienne. Cut the fennel bulb in half and cut out the hard core. Cut into slices, then cut the slices into julienne.

3 Heat the remaining oil in a wok or frying pan until very hot. Add all the vegetables, including the chilli, and stir-fry for 7–8 minutes.

4 Add the ginger and garlic and stir-fry for 2 minutes, then add the spices. Cook for 1 minute. Add the spring onions and stir-fry for 1 minute. Pour in the warm water and cook for 1 minute. Stir in the noodles and toss well together. Serve sprinkled with sliced red chilli, if liked.

Mushroom Bolognese

A quick – and exceedingly tasty – vegetarian version of the classic Italian meat dish.

Serves 4

INGREDIENTS
450 g/1 lb mushrooms
15 ml/1 tbsp olive oil
1 onion, chopped
1 garlic clove, crushed
15 ml/1 tbsp tomato purée
400 g/14 oz can chopped tomatoes
15 ml/1 tbsp chopped fresh oregano
450 g/1 lb fresh pasta
Parmesan cheese, to serve
chopped fresh oregano, to garnish

mushrooms

chopped tomatoes

oregano

garlic
clove

pasta

onion

Parmesan
cheese

tomato
purée

1 Trim the mushroom stems neatly, then cut each mushroom into quarters.

2 Heat the oil in a large pan. Add the chopped onion and garlic and cook for 2–3 minutes.

3 Add the mushrooms to the pan and cook over a high heat for 3–4 minutes, stirring occasionally.

4 Stir in the tomato purée, chopped tomatoes and oregano. Lower the heat, cover and cook for 5 minutes.

5 Meanwhile, bring a large pan of salted water to the boil. Cook the pasta for 2–3 minutes until just tender.

COOK'S TIP
If you prefer to use dried pasta, make this the first thing that you cook. It will take 10–12 minutes, during which time you can make the mushroom mixture. Use 350 g/12 oz dried pasta.

6 Season the bolognese sauce with salt and pepper. Drain the pasta, tip it into a bowl and add the mushroom mixture. Toss to mix. Serve in individual bowls, topped with shavings of fresh Parmesan cheese and a sprinkling of chopped fresh oregano.

Fried Noodles with Beansprouts and Asparagus

Soft fried noodles contrast beautifully with crisp beansprouts and asparagus.

Serves 2

INGREDIENTS

115 g/4 oz dried egg noodles
60 ml/4 tbsp vegetable oil
1 small onion, chopped
2.5 cm/1 in piece of fresh root
  ginger, peeled and grated
2 garlic cloves, crushed
175 g/6 oz young asparagus
  spears, trimmed
115 g/4 oz beansprouts
4 spring onions, sliced
45 ml/3 tbsp soy sauce
salt and freshly ground black pepper

onion

spring onions

garlic cloves

root ginger

soy sauce

beansprouts

egg noodles

asparagus spears

1 Bring a pan of salted water to the boil. Add the noodles and cook for 2–3 minutes, until just tender. Drain and toss in 30 ml/2 tbsp of the oil.

2 Heat the remaining oil in a wok or frying pan until very hot. Add the onion, ginger and garlic and stir-fry for 2–3 minutes. Add the asparagus and stir-fry for a further 2–3 minutes.

3 Add the noodles and beansprouts and stir-fry for 2 minutes.

4 Stir in the spring onions and soy sauce. Season to taste, adding salt sparingly as the soy sauce will add quite a salty flavour. Stir-fry for 1 minute, then serve at once.

Pasta with Coriander and Grilled Aubergines

Pasta with a piquant sauce of coriander and lime – a variation on the classic pesto – is superb served with grilled aubergines.

Serves 2

INGREDIENTS
15 g/¹/₂ oz coriander leaves
30 ml/2 tbsp pine nuts
30 ml/2 tbsp freshly grated
  Parmesan cheese
3 garlic cloves
juice of ¹/₂ lime
105 ml/7 tbsp olive oil
225 g/8 oz dried cellentani or other
  pasta shapes
1 large aubergine
salt and freshly ground black pepper

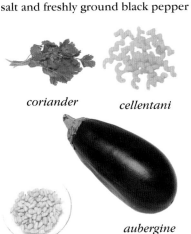
coriander   cellentani

aubergine

pine nuts

Parmesan cheese   garlic cloves   lime

1 Process the coriander leaves, pine nuts, Parmesan, garlic, lime juice and 60 ml/4 tbsp of the olive oil in a food processor or blender for 30 seconds until almost smooth. Bring a pan of salted water to the boil, add the pasta and cook for 10–12 minutes until cooked but firm to the bite.

2 Meanwhile, cut the aubergine in half lengthways, then cut each half into 5 mm/¹/₄ in slices. Spread out on a baking sheet, brush with the remaining oil and season well with salt and black pepper.

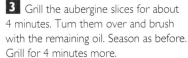

3 Grill the aubergine slices for about 4 minutes. Turn them over and brush with the remaining oil. Season as before. Grill for 4 minutes more.

4 Drain the pasta, tip it into a bowl and toss with the coriander sauce. Serve with the grilled aubergine slices.

Spring Vegetable Stir-fry

A colourful, dazzling medley of fresh and sweet young vegetables.

Serves 4

INGREDIENTS
15 ml/1 tbsp peanut oil
1 garlic clove, sliced
2.5 cm/1 in piece of fresh ginger root, finely chopped
115 g/4 oz baby carrots
115 g/4 oz patty pan squash
115 g/4 oz baby sweetcorn
115 g/4 oz French beans, topped and tailed
115 g/4 oz sugar-snap peas, topped and tailed
115 g/4 oz young asparagus, cut into 7.5 cm/3 in pieces
8 spring onions, trimmed and cut into 5 cm/2 in pieces
115 g/4 oz cherry tomatoes

FOR THE DRESSING
juice of 2 limes
15 ml/1 tbsp runny honey
15 ml/1 tbsp soy sauce
5 ml/1 tsp sesame oil

1 Heat the peanut oil in a wok or large frying pan.

2 Add the garlic and ginger and stir-fry over a high heat for 1 minute.

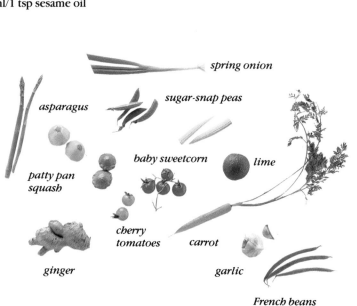

3 Add the carrots, patty pan squash, sweetcorn and beans and stir-fry for another 3–4 minutes.

4 Add the sugar-snap peas, asparagus, spring onions and cherry tomatoes and stir-fry for a further 1–2 minutes.

spring onion

asparagus

sugar-snap peas

patty pan squash

baby sweetcorn

lime

ginger

cherry tomatoes

carrot

garlic

French beans

5 Mix the dressing ingredients together and add to the pan.

6 Stir well then cover the pan. Cook for 2–3 minutes more until the vegetables are just tender but still crisp.

COOK'S TIP
Stir-fries take only moments to cook so prepare this dish at the last minute.

Spinach and Potato Galette

Creamy layers of potato, spinach and herbs make a
warming supper dish.

Serves 6

INGREDIENTS

900 g/2 lb large potatoes
450 g/1 lb fresh spinach
2 eggs
400 g/14 oz/1¾ cup low-fat cream
   cheese
15 ml/1 tbsp grainy mustard
50 g/2 oz chopped fresh herbs
   (e.g. chives, parsley, chervil or
   sorrel)
salt and freshly ground black pepper

mustard

parsley

cream
cheese

spinach

egg

potatoes

chives

cherry tomatoes

chervil

sorrel

1 Preheat the oven to 180°C/350°F/ Gas 4. Line a deep 23 cm/9 in cake tin with non-stick baking paper. Place the potatoes in a large pan and cover with cold water. Bring to the boil and cook for 10 minutes. Drain well and allow to cool slightly before slicing thinly.

2 Wash the spinach and place in a large pan with only the water that is clinging to the leaves. Cover and cook, stirring once, until the spinach has just wilted. Drain well in a sieve and squeeze out the excess moisture. Chop finely.

3 Beat the eggs with the cream cheese and mustard then stir in the chopped spinach and fresh herbs.

4 Place a layer of the sliced potatoes in the lined tin, arranging them in concentric circles. Top with a spoonful of the cream cheese mixture and spread out. Continue layering, seasoning with salt and pepper as you go, until all the potatoes and the cream cheese mixture are used up.

5 Cover the tin with a piece of foil and place in a roasting tin.

6 Fill the roasting tin with enough boiling water to come halfway up the sides, and cook in the oven for 45–50 minutes. Turn out onto a plate and serve hot or cold.

COOK'S TIP

Choose firm potatoes for this dish
such as Cara, Desirée or Estima.

Grilled Mixed Peppers with Feta and Green Salsa

Soft smoky grilled peppers make a lovely combination with the slightly tart salsa.

Serves 4

INGREDIENTS

4 medium peppers in different
  colours
45 ml/3 tbsp chopped fresh flat-leaf
  parsley
45 ml/3 tbsp chopped fresh dill
45 ml/3 tbsp chopped fresh mint
½ small red onion, finely chopped
15 ml/1 tbsp capers, coarsely chopped
50 g/2 oz/¼ cup Greek olives, pitted
  and sliced
1 fresh green chilli, seeded and finely
  chopped
60 g/4 tbsp pistachios, chopped
75 ml/5 tbsp extra-virgin olive oil
45 ml/3 tbsp fresh lime juice
115 g/4 oz/½ cup medium-fat feta
  cheese, crumbled
25 g/1 oz gherkins, finely chopped

olives

feta cheese

green chilli

mint

pistachios

peppers

gherkins

red onion

1 Preheat the grill. Place the whole peppers on a tray and grill until charred and blistered.

2 Place the peppers in a plastic bag and leave to cool.

COOK'S TIP

Feta cheese is quite salty so if preferred, soak in cold water and drain well before using.

3 Peel, seed and cut the peppers into even strips.

4 Mix all the remaining ingredients together, and stir in the pepper strips.

Beetroot and Celeriac Gratin

Beautiful ruby-red slices of beetroot and celeriac make a stunning light accompaniment to any main course dish.

Serves 6

INGREDIENTS
350 g/12 oz raw beetroot
350 g/12 oz celeriac
4 thyme sprigs
6 juniper berries, crushed
salt and freshly ground black pepper
100 ml/4 fl oz/½ cup fresh orange juice
100 ml/4 fl oz/½ cup vegetable stock

celeriac

orange juice

juniper berries

beetroot

thyme

1 Preheat the oven to 190°C/375°F/Gas 5. Peel and slice the beetroot very finely. Quarter and peel the celeriac and slice very finely.

2 Fill a 25 cm/10 in diameter, cast iron, ovenproof or flameproof frying pan with alternate layers of beetroot and celeriac slices, sprinkling with the thyme, juniper and seasoning between each layer.

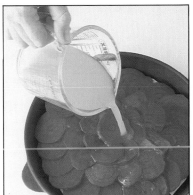

3 Mix the orange juice and stock together and pour over the gratin. Place over a medium heat and bring to the boil. Boil for 2 minutes.

4 Cover with foil and place in the oven for 15–20 minutes. Remove the foil and raise the oven temperature to 200°C/400°F/Gas 6. Cook for a further 10 minutes.

Aubergine, Roast Garlic and Red Pepper Pâté

This is a simple pâté of smoky baked aubergine, sweet pink peppercorns and red peppers, with more than a hint of garlic!

Serves 4

INGREDIENTS
3 medium aubergines
2 red peppers
5 whole garlic cloves
7.5 ml/1½ tsp pink peppercorns in brine, drained and crushed
30 ml/2 tbsp chopped fresh coriander

aubergine

garlic

coriander

pink peppercorns

red pepper

1 Preheat the oven to 200°C/400°F/Gas 6. Arrange the whole aubergines, peppers and garlic cloves on a baking sheet and place in the oven. After 10 minutes remove the garlic cloves and turn over the aubergines and peppers.

2 Peel the garlic cloves and place in the bowl of a blender.

3 After a further 20 minutes remove the blistered and charred peppers from the oven and place in a plastic bag. Leave to cool.

4 After a further 10 minutes remove the aubergines from the oven. Split in half and scoop the flesh into a sieve placed over a bowl. Press the flesh with a spoon to remove the bitter juices.

5 Add the mixture to the garlic in the blender and blend until smooth. Place in a large mixing bowl.

6 Peel and chop the red peppers and stir into the aubergine mixture. Mix in the peppercorns and fresh coriander and serve at once.

Courgettes and Asparagus en Papillote

An impressive dinner party accompaniment, these puffed paper parcels should be broken open at the table by each guest, so that the wonderful aroma can be fully appreciated.

Serves 4

INGREDIENTS
2 medium courgettes
1 medium leek
225 g/8 oz young asparagus, trimmed
4 tarragon sprigs
4 whole garlic cloves, unpeeled
salt and freshly ground black pepper
1 egg, beaten

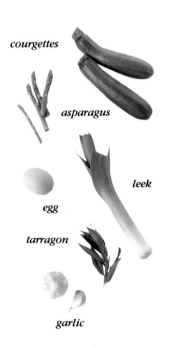

courgettes

asparagus

leek

egg

tarragon

garlic

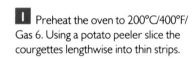

1 Preheat the oven to 200°C/400°F/Gas 6. Using a potato peeler slice the courgettes lengthwise into thin strips.

2 Cut the leek into very fine julienne strips and cut the asparagus evenly into 5 cm/2 in lengths.

3 Cut out 4 sheets of greaseproof paper measuring 30 × 38 cm/12 × 15 in and fold in half. Draw a large curve to make a heart shape when unfolded. Cut along the inside of the line and open out.

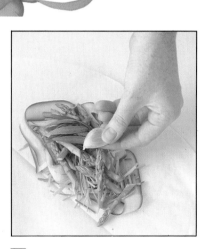

4 Divide the courgettes, asparagus and leek evenly between each paper heart, positioning the filling on one side of the fold line, and topping each with a sprig of tarragon and an unpeeled garlic clove. Season to taste.

COOK'S TIP

Experiment with other vegetables and herbs such as sugar-snap peas and mint or baby carrots and rosemary. The possibilities are endless.

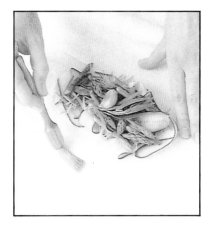

5 Brush the edges lightly with the beaten egg and fold over.

6 Pleat the edges together so that each parcel is completely sealed. Lay the parcels on a baking tray and cook for 10 minutes. Serve immediately.

Broccoli and Chestnut Terrine

Served hot or cold, this versatile terrine is equally suitable for a dinner party as for a picnic.

Serves 4–6

INGREDIENTS

450 g/1 lb broccoli, cut into small florets
225 g/8 oz cooked chestnuts, roughly chopped
50 g/2 oz/1 cup fresh wholemeal breadcrumbs
60 ml/4 tbsp low-fat natural yogurt
30 ml/2 tbsp Parmesan cheese, finely grated
salt, grated nutmeg and freshly ground black pepper
2 eggs, beaten

yogurt

breadcrumbs

broccoli

chestnuts

egg

Parmesan

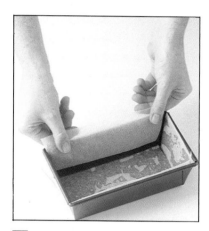

1 Preheat the oven to 180°C/350°F/ Gas 4. Line a 900 g/2 lb loaf tin with non-stick baking paper.

2 Blanch or steam the broccoli for 3–4 minutes until just tender. Drain well. Reserve ¼ of the smallest florets and chop the rest finely.

3 Mix together the chestnuts, breadcrumbs, yogurt and Parmesan, and season to taste.

4 Fold in the chopped broccoli, reserved florets and the beaten eggs.

5 Spoon the broccoli mixture into the prepared tin.

6 Place in a roasting tin and pour in boiling water to come halfway up the sides of the loaf tin. Bake for 20–25 minutes. Remove from the oven and tip out onto a plate or tray. Serve cut into even slices.

Baked Squash

A creamy, sweet and nutty filling makes the perfect topping for tender buttery squash.

Serves 4

INGREDIENTS
2 butternut or acorn squash, 500 g/
  1¼ lb each
15 ml/1 tbsp olive oil
175 g/6 oz/¾ cup canned sweetcorn
  kernels, drained
115 g/4 oz/½ cup unsweetened
  chestnut purée
75 ml/5 tbsp low-fat yogurt
salt and freshly ground black pepper
50 g/2 oz/¼ cup fresh goat's cheese
snipped chives, to garnish

yogurt

chestnut purée

sweetcorn

butternut squash

goat's cheese

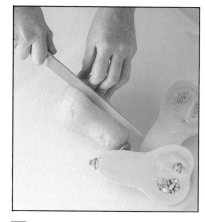

1 Preheat the oven to 180°C/350°F/Gas 4. Cut the squash in half lengthwise.

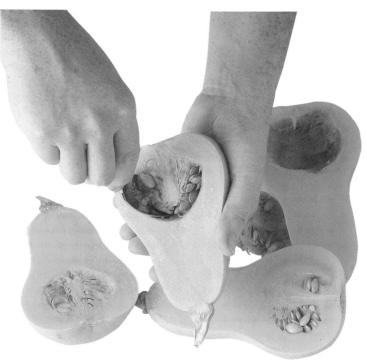

2 Scoop out the seeds with a spoon and discard.

3 Place the squash halves on a baking sheet and brush the flesh lightly with the oil. Bake in the oven for 30 minutes.

4 Mix together the sweetcorn, chestnut purée and yogurt in a bowl. Season to taste.

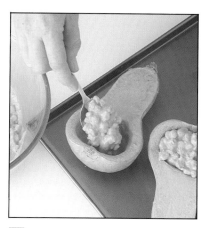

5 Remove the squash from the oven and divide the chestnut mixture between them, spooning it into the hollows.

COOK'S TIP

Use mozzarella or other mild, soft cheeses in place of goat's cheese. The cheese can be omitted entirely for a lower-fat alternative.

6 Top each half with ¼ of the goat's cheese and return to the oven for a further 10–15 minutes. Garnish with snipped chives.

Red Cabbage in Port and Red Wine

A sweet and sour, spicy red cabbage dish, with the added crunch of pears and walnuts.

Serves 6

INGREDIENTS

15 ml/1 tbsp walnut oil
1 onion, sliced
2 whole star anise
5 ml/1 tsp ground cinnamon
pinch of ground cloves
450 g/1 lb red cabbage, finely
    shredded
25 g/1 oz/2 tbsp dark brown sugar
45 ml/3 tbsp red wine vinegar
300 ml/½ pint/1¼ cups red wine
150 ml/¼ pint/⅔ cup port
2 pears, cut into 1 cm/½ in cubes
115 g/4 oz/½ cup raisins
salt and freshly ground black pepper
115 g/4 oz/½ cup walnut halves

brown sugar

red cabbage

pears

onion   raisins

walnut halves

star anise

red wine vinegar

port

red wine

1 Heat the oil in a large pan. Add the onion and cook gently for about 5 minutes until softened.

2 Add the star anise, cinnamon, cloves and cabbage and cook for about 3 minutes more.

3 Stir in the sugar, vinegar, red wine and port. Cover the pan and simmer gently for 10 minutes, stirring occasionally.

4 Stir in the cubed pears and raisins and cook for a further 10 minutes or until the cabbage is tender. Season to taste. Mix in the walnut halves and serve.

Leek and Caraway Gratin with a Carrot Crust

Tender leeks are mixed with a creamy caraway sauce and a crunchy carrot topping.

Serves 4–6

INGREDIENTS
675 g/1½ lb leeks, cut into 5 cm/2 in pieces
150 ml/¼ pint/⅔ cup vegetable stock or water
45 ml/3 tbsp dry white wine
5 ml/1 tsp caraway seeds
pinch of salt
275 ml/10 fl oz skimmed milk as required
25 g/1 oz/2 tbsp butter
25 g/1 oz/¼ cup plain flour

FOR THE TOPPING
115 g/4 oz/2 cups fresh wholemeal breadcrumbs
115 g/4 oz/2 cups grated carrot
30 ml/2 tbsp chopped fresh parsley
75 g/3 oz Jarlsberg cheese, coarsely grated
25 g/1 oz/2 tbsp slivered almonds

parsley

vegetable stock

Jarlsberg

leek

breadcrumbs

butter

1 Place the leeks in a large pan. Add the stock or water, wine, caraway seeds and salt. Bring to a simmer, cover and cook for 5–7 minutes until the leeks are just tender.

2 With a slotted spoon, transfer the leeks to an ovenproof dish. Reduce the remaining liquid to half then make the amount up to 350 ml/12 fl oz/1½ cups with skimmed milk.

3 Preheat the oven to 180°C/350°F/ Gas 4. Melt the butter in a saucepan, stir in the flour and cook without allowing it to colour for 1–2 minutes. Gradually add the stock and milk, stirring well after each addition, until you have a smooth sauce. Simmer for 5–6 minutes then pour over the leeks in the dish.

4 Mix all the topping ingredients together in a bowl and sprinkle over the leeks. Bake for 20–25 minutes until golden.

Mushroom and Okra Curry with Fresh Mango Relish

This simple but delicious curry with its fresh gingery mango relish is best served with plain basmati rice.

Serves 4

INGREDIENTS
4 garlic cloves, roughly chopped
2.5 cm/1 in piece of fresh ginger root, peeled and roughly chopped
1–2 red chillies, seeded and chopped
175 ml/6 fl oz/¾ cup cold water
15 ml/1 tbsp sunflower oil
5 ml/1 tsp coriander seeds
5 ml/1 tsp cumin seeds
5 ml/1 tsp ground cumin
2 green cardamom pods, seeds removed and ground
pinch of ground turmeric
1 × 400 g/14 oz can chopped tomatoes
450 g/1 lb mushrooms, quartered if large
225 g/8 oz okra, trimmed and cut into 1 cm/½ in slices
30 ml/2 tbsp chopped fresh coriander
basmati rice, to serve

FOR THE MANGO RELISH
1 large ripe mango, about 500 g/1¼ lb in weight
1 small garlic clove, crushed
1 onion, finely chopped
10 ml/2 tsp grated fresh ginger root
1 fresh red chilli, seeded and finely chopped
pinch of salt and sugar

1 For the mango relish, peel the mango and cut off the flesh from the stone.

2 In a bowl mash the mango flesh with a fork or pulse in a food processor, and mix in the rest of the relish ingredients. Set to one side.

3 Place the garlic, ginger, chilli and 45 ml/3 tbsp of the water into a blender and blend until smooth.

4 Heat the sunflower oil in a large pan. Add the whole coriander and cumin seeds and allow them to sizzle for a few seconds. Add the ground cumin, ground cardamom and turmeric and cook for 1 minute more.

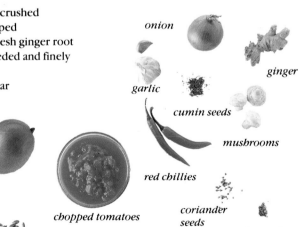

onion
ginger
garlic
cumin seeds
mushrooms
mango
red chillies
okra
coriander seeds
chopped tomatoes
turmeric
cardamom pods

5 Add the paste from the blender, the tomatoes, remaining water, mushrooms and okra. Stir to mix well and bring to the boil. Reduce the heat, cover, and simmer for 5 minutes.

6 Remove the cover, turn up the heat slightly and cook for another 5–10 minutes until the okra is tender. Stir in the fresh coriander and serve with rice and the mango relish.

Potato Gnocchi with Hazelnut Sauce

These delicate potato dumplings are dressed with a creamy hazelnut sauce.

Serves 4

INGREDIENTS
675 g/1½ lb large potatoes
115 g/4 oz/1 cup plain flour

FOR THE HAZELNUT SAUCE
115 g/4 oz/½ cup hazelnuts, roasted
1 garlic clove, roughly chopped
½ tsp grated lemon rind
½ tsp lemon juice
30 ml/2 tbsp sunflower oil
150 g/5 oz/scant ¾ cup low-fat
    fromage blanc
salt and freshly ground black pepper

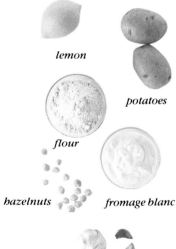

lemon

potatoes

flour

hazelnuts   *fromage blanc*

garlic

1 Place 65 g/2½ oz of the hazelnuts in a blender with the garlic, grated lemon rind and juice. Blend until coarsely chopped. Gradually add the oil and blend until smooth. Spoon into a bowl and mix in the fromage blanc. Season to taste.

2 Place the potatoes in a pan of cold water. Bring to the boil and cook for 20–25 minutes. Drain well in a colander.

When cool, peel and purée the potatoes whilst still warm by passing them through a food mill into a bowl.

3 Add the flour a little at a time (you may not need all the flour as potatoes vary in texture). Stop adding flour when the mixture is smooth and slightly sticky. Add salt to taste.

4 Roll out the mixture onto a floured board, into a long sausage about 1 cm/½ in in diameter. Cut into 2 cm/¾ in lengths.

5 Take 1 piece at a time and press it on to a floured fork. Roll each piece slightly while pressing it along the prongs and off the fork. Flip onto a floured plate or tray. Continue with the rest of the mixture.

COOK'S TIP
A light touch is the key to making soft gnocchi, so handle the dough as little as possible to prevent the mixture from becoming tough.

6 Bring a large pan of water to the boil and drop in 20–25 pieces at a time. They will rise to the surface very quickly. Let them cook for 10–15 seconds more, then lift them out with a slotted spoon. Drop into a dish and keep warm. Continue with the rest of the gnocchi. To heat the sauce, place in a heatproof bowl over a pan of simmering water and heat gently, being careful not to let the sauce curdle. Pour the sauce over the gnocchi. Roughly chop the remaining hazelnuts and scatter over the sauce.

Asparagus Rolls with Herb Butter Sauce

For a taste sensation, try tender asparagus spears wrapped in crisp filo pastry. The buttery herb sauce makes the perfect accompaniment.

Serves 2

INGREDIENTS
4 sheets of filo pastry
50 g/2 oz/¼ cup butter, melted
16 young asparagus spears, trimmed

FOR THE SAUCE
2 shallots, finely chopped
1 bay leaf
150 ml/¼ pint/⅔ cup dry white wine
175 g/6 oz butter, softened
15 ml/1 tbsp chopped fresh herbs
salt and freshly ground black pepper
snipped chives, to garnish

fresh herbs

chives

dry white wine

asparagus spears

filo pastry   *butter*

bay leaf   *shallots*

1 Preheat the oven to 200°C/400°F/ Gas 6. Brush each filo sheet with melted butter. Fold one corner of the sheet down to the bottom edge to give a wedge shape.

2 Lay 4 asparagus spears on top at the longest edge and roll up towards the shortest edge. Using the remaining filo and asparagus spears make 3 more rolls in the same way.

3 Lay the rolls on a greased baking sheet. Brush with the remaining melted butter. Bake in the oven for 8 minutes until golden.

4 Meanwhile, put the shallots, bay leaf and wine into a pan. Cover and cook over a high heat until the wine is reduced to about 45–60 ml/3–4 tbsp.

5 Strain the wine mixture into a bowl. Whisk in the butter, a little at a time, until the sauce is smooth and glossy.

6 Stir in the herbs and add salt and pepper to taste. Return to the pan and keep the sauce warm. Serve the rolls on individual plates with a salad garnish, if liked. Serve the butter sauce separately, sprinkled with a few snipped chives.

Tomato Omelette Envelopes

Delicious chive omelettes, folded and filled with tomato and melting Camembert cheese.

Serves 2

INGREDIENTS
1 small onion
4 tomatoes
30 ml/2 tbsp vegetable oil
4 eggs
30 ml/2 tbsp snipped fresh chives
115 g/4 oz Camembert cheese,
  rinded and diced
salt and freshly ground black pepper

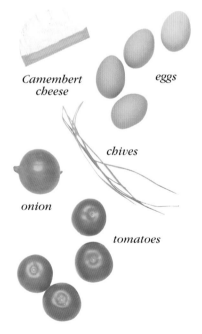

Camembert
cheese

eggs

chives

onion

tomatoes

1 Cut the onion in half. Cut each half into thin wedges. Cut the tomatoes into wedges of similar size.

2 Heat 15 ml/1 tbsp of the oil in a frying pan. Cook the onion for 2 minutes over a moderate heat, then raise the heat and add the tomatoes. Cook for a further 2 minutes, then remove the pan from the heat.

3 Beat the eggs with the chives in a bowl. Add salt and pepper to taste. Heat the remaining oil in an omelette pan. Add half the egg mixture and tilt the pan to spread thinly. Cook for 1 minute.

4 Flip the omelette over and cook for 1 minute more. Remove from the pan and keep hot. Make a second omelette with the remaining egg mixture.

5 Return the tomato mixture to a high heat. Add the cheese and toss the mixture over the heat for 1 minute.

6 Divide the mixture between the omelettes and fold them over. Serve at once. Add crisp lettuce leaves and chunks of Granary bread, if liked.

COOK'S TIP
You may need to wipe the pan clean between the omelettes and reheat a little more oil.

Mushrooms with Leeks and Stilton

Upturned mushrooms make perfect containers for this leek and Stilton filling.

Serves 2–3

INGREDIENTS
1 leek, thinly sliced
6 flat mushrooms
2 garlic cloves, crushed
30 ml/2 tbsp chopped fresh parsley
115 g/4 oz/½ cup butter, softened
115 g/4 oz Stilton cheese
freshly ground black pepper
frisée and tomato halves, to garnish

leek

butter

flat mushrooms

parsley

Stilton cheese

garlic cloves

1 Put the leek slices in a small pan with a little water. Cover and cook for about 5 minutes until tender. Drain, refresh under cold water and drain again.

2 Remove the stalks from the mushrooms and set them aside. Put the mushroom caps, hollows uppermost, on an oiled baking sheet.

3 Put the mushroom stalks, garlic and parsley in a food processor or blender. Process for 1 minute. Tip into a bowl, add the leek and butter and season with freshly ground black pepper to taste. Preheat the grill.

4 Crumble the Stilton into the mushroom mixture and mix well. Divide the Stilton mixture between the mushroom caps and grill for 6–7 minutes until bubbling. Serve garnished with frisée and halved tomatoes.

Tomato and Okra Stew

Okra is an unusual and delicious vegetable. It releases a sticky sap when cooked, which helps to thicken the stew.

Serves 4

INGREDIENTS
15 ml/1 tbsp olive oil
1 onion, chopped
400 g/14 oz can pimientos, drained
2 x 400 g/14 oz cans chopped
  tomatoes
275 g/10 oz okra
30 ml/2 tbsp chopped fresh parsley
salt and freshly ground black pepper

parsley

chopped tomatoes

pimientos

onion

okra

1 Heat the oil in a pan. Add the onion and cook for 2–3 minutes.

2 Roughly chop the pimientos and add to the onion. Add the chopped tomatoes and mix well.

3 Cut the tops off the okra and cut into halves or quarters if large. Add to the tomato sauce in the pan. Season with plenty of salt and pepper.

4 Bring the vegetable stew to the boil, then lower the heat, cover the pan and simmer for 12 minutes until the vegetables are tender and the sauce has thickened. Stir in the chopped parsley and serve at once.

Vegetable Kebabs with Mustard and Honey

A colourful mixture of vegetables and tofu, skewered, glazed and grilled until tender.

Serves 4

INGREDIENTS
1 yellow pepper
2 small courgettes
225 g/8 oz piece of firm tofu
8 cherry tomatoes
8 button mushrooms
15 ml/1 tbsp wholegrain mustard
15 ml/1 tbsp clear honey
30 ml/2 tbsp olive oil
salt and freshly ground black pepper

TO SERVE
4 portions cooked mixed rice
  and wild rice
lime segments
flat leaf parsley

1 Cut the pepper in half and remove the seeds. Cut each half into quarters and cut each quarter in half.

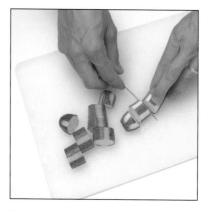

2 Top and tail the courgettes and peel them decoratively, if you like. Cut each courgette into 8 chunks.

3 Cut the tofu into pieces of a similar size to the vegetables.

courgettes

cherry tomatoes

yellow pepper

clear honey

tofu

wholegrain mustard

button mushrooms

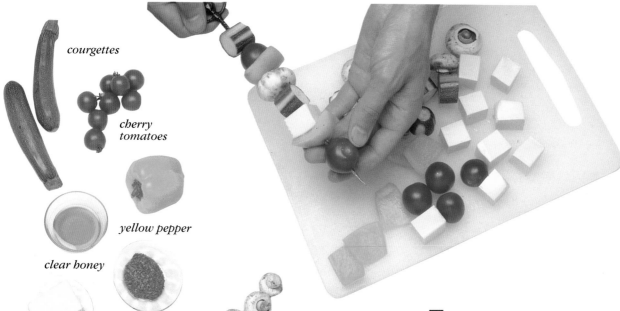

5 Whisk the mustard, honey and olive oil in a small bowl. Add salt and pepper to taste.

4 Thread the pepper pieces, courgette chunks, tofu, cherry tomatoes and mushrooms alternately on to four metal or bamboo skewers. Preheat the grill.

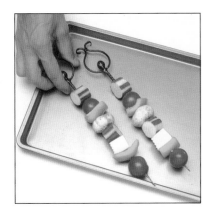

6 Put the kebabs on to a baking sheet. Brush with the mustard and honey glaze. Cook under the grill for 8 minutes, turning once or twice during cooking. Serve with a mixture of long grain and wild rice, and garnish with lime segments and parsley.

COOK'S TIP
If using bamboo skewers, soak them in a bowl of cold water before threading, to prevent them burning when placed under the grill.

Deep-fried Florets with Tangy Thyme Mayonnaise

Cauliflower and broccoli make a sensational snack when coated in a beer batter and deep-fried. Serve with a tangy mayonnaise.

Serves 2–3

INGREDIENTS
175 g/6 oz cauliflower
175 g/6 oz broccoli
2 eggs, separated
30 ml/2 tbsp olive oil
250 ml/8 fl oz/1 cup beer
150 ml/5 oz/1¼ cups plain flour
pinch of salt
30 ml/2 tbsp shredded fresh basil
vegetable oil for deep-frying
150 ml/¼ pint/⅔ cup good quality
  mayonnaise
10 ml/2 tsp chopped fresh thyme
10 ml/2 tsp grated lemon rind
10 ml/2 tsp lemon juice
sea salt, for sprinkling

eggs
basil
plain flour
mayonnaise
broccoli
cauliflower
beer
thyme
lemon

1 Break the cauliflower and broccoli into small florets, cutting large florets into smaller pieces. Set aside.

2 Beat the egg yolks, olive oil, beer, flour and salt in a bowl. Strain the batter if necessary, to remove any lumps.

3 Whisk the egg whites until stiff. Fold into the batter with the basil.

4 Heat the oil for deep-frying to 180°C/350°F or until a cube of bread, when added to the oil, browns in 30–45 seconds. Dip the florets in the batter and deep-fry in batches for 2–3 minutes until the coating is golden and crisp. Drain on kitchen paper.

5 Mix the mayonnaise, thyme, lemon rind and juice in a small bowl.

6 Sprinkle the florets with sea salt. Serve with the thyme and lemon mayonnaise.

Black Bean and Vegetable Stir-fry

The secret of a quick stir-fry is to prepare all the ingredients first. This colourful vegetable mixture is coated in a classic Chinese sauce.

Serves 4

INGREDIENTS
8 spring onions
225 g/8 oz/2 cups button
  mushrooms
1 red pepper
1 green pepper
2 large carrots
60 ml/4 tbsp sesame oil
2 garlic cloves, crushed
60 ml/4 tbsp black bean sauce
90 ml/6 tbsp warm water
225 g/8 oz beansprouts
salt and freshly ground black pepper

1 Thinly slice the spring onions and button mushrooms.

2 Cut both the peppers in half, remove the seeds and slice the flesh into thin strips.

spring onions

black bean sauce

sesame oil

button mushrooms

red pepper

beansprouts

carrots

garlic cloves

onion

green pepper

3 Cut the carrots in half. Cut each half into thin strips lengthways. Stack the slices and cut through them to make very fine strips.

4 Heat the oil in a large wok or frying pan until very hot. Add the spring onions and garlic and stir-fry for 30 seconds.

5 Add the mushrooms, peppers and carrots. Stir-fry for 5–6 minutes over a high heat until the vegetables are just beginning to soften.

6 Mix the black bean sauce with the water. Add to the wok or pan and cook for 3–4 minutes. Stir in the beansprouts and stir-fry for 1 minute more, until all the vegetables are coated in the sauce. Season to taste. Serve at once.

COOK'S TIP
For best results the oil in the wok must be very hot before adding the vegetables.

Brioche with Mixed Mushrooms

Mushrooms in a rich sherry sauce, served on toasted brioche, make a delectable lunch, but would also serve 6 as a starter.

Serves 4

INGREDIENTS

75 g/3 oz/6 tbsp butter
1 vegetable stock cube
450 g/1 lb shiitake mushrooms, caps only, sliced
225 g/8 oz button mushrooms, sliced
45 ml/3 tbsp dry sherry
250 ml/8 fl oz/1 cup crème fraîche
10 ml/2 tsp lemon juice
8 thick slices of brioche
salt and freshly ground black pepper

shiitake and button mushrooms

brioche

butter

stock cube

crème fraîche

lemon

COOK'S TIP
If shiitake mushrooms are too expensive or not available, substitute more button or brown cap mushrooms. Wipe the mushrooms with kitchen paper before use.

1 Melt the butter in a large pan. Crumble in the stock cube and stir for about 30 seconds.

2 Add the shiitake and button mushrooms to the pan and cook for 5 minutes over a moderate to high heat, stirring occasionally.

3 Stir in the sherry. Cook for 1 minute, then add the crème fraîche. Cook, stirring, over a gentle heat for 5 minutes. Stir in the lemon juice and add salt and pepper to taste. Preheat the grill.

4 Toast the brioche slices under the grill until just golden on both sides. Spoon the mushrooms on top, flash briefly under the grill, and serve. Fresh thyme may be used to garnish, if liked.

Ciabatta Rolls with Courgettes and Saffron

Split crunchy ciabatta rolls are filled with courgettes in a creamy tomato sauce flavoured with saffron. Use a mixture of green and yellow courgettes if possible.

Serves 4

INGREDIENTS
675 g/1½ lb small courgettes
15 ml/1 tbsp olive oil
2 shallots, freshly chopped
4 ciabatta rolls
200 g/7 oz can chopped tomatoes
pinch of sugar
a few saffron threads
50 ml/2 fl oz/¼ cup single cream
salt and freshly ground black pepper

courgettes

chopped tomatoes

saffron

shallots

ciabatta rolls   *single cream*

COOK'S TIP
To avoid heating your oven, heat the rolls in a microwave. Put them on a plate, cover with kitchen paper and heat on HIGH for 30–45 seconds.

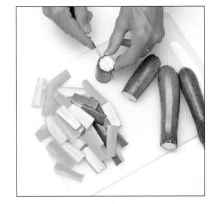

1 Preheat the oven to 180°C/350°F/ Gas 4. Top and tail the courgettes. Then, using a sharp knife, cut them into 4 cm/1½ in lengths, then cut each piece into quarters lengthways.

2 Heat the oil in a large frying pan. Add the shallots and fry over a moderate heat for 1–2 minutes. Put the rolls into the oven to warm through.

3 Add the courgettes to the shallots, mix well and cook for 6 minutes, stirring frequently, until just beginning to soften.

4 Stir in the tomatoes and sugar. Steep the saffron threads in a little hot water for a few minutes, then add to the pan with the cream. Cook for 4 minutes, stirring occasionally. Season to taste. Split open the rolls and fill with the courgettes and sauce.

Potato, Broccoli and Red Pepper Stir-fry

A hot and hearty stir-fry of vegetables with just a hint of fresh ginger.

Serves 2

INGREDIENTS
450 g/1 lb potatoes
45 ml/3 tbsp groundnut oil
50 g/2 oz/¼ cup butter
1 small onion, chopped
1 red pepper, seeded and chopped
225 g/8 oz broccoli, broken
  into florets
2.5 cm/1 in piece of fresh root
  ginger, peeled and grated
salt and freshly ground black pepper

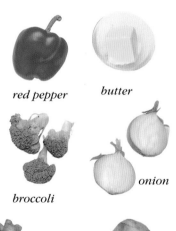

red pepper   butter

broccoli   onion

root ginger   potatoes

COOK'S TIP

Although a wok is the preferred pan for stir-frying, for this recipe a flat frying pan is best to cook the potatoes quickly.

1 Peel the potatoes and cut them into 1 cm/½ in dice.

2 Heat the oil in a large frying pan and add the potatoes. Cook for 8 minutes over a high heat, stirring and tossing occasionally, until the potatoes are browned and just tender.

3 Drain off the oil. Add the butter to the potatoes in the pan. As soon as it melts, add the onion and red pepper. Stir-fry for 2 minutes.

4 Add the broccoli florets and ginger to the pan. Stir-fry for 2–3 minutes more, taking care not to break up the potatoes. Add salt and pepper to taste and serve at once.

Bubble and Squeak with Fried Eggs

Next time you are serving mashed potato, make double the amount and chill half so that you can make this tasty dish the next day.

Serves 2

INGREDIENTS
½ Savoy cabbage
50 g/2 oz/¼ cup butter
1 small onion, finely chopped
450 g/1 lb mashed potato
15 ml/1 tbsp chopped fresh parsley
15 ml/1 tbsp vegetable oil
2 eggs
salt and freshly ground black pepper
2 tomatoes, halved, to serve

eggs

mashed potato

butter

onion

Savoy cabbage

parsley

1 Cut out and discard the hard core of the cabbage. Strip off and discard the outer layer of leaves. Finely slice the remaining cabbage and set aside.

2 Melt the butter in a large frying pan. Add the onion and fry for 2–3 minutes until just tender. Reduce the heat slightly, add the cabbage and cook, stirring constantly, for 2–3 minutes.

3 Add the mashed potato to the pan. Stir to combine. Cook for 5–6 minutes until the mixture starts to brown. Stir in the chopped parsley and add salt and pepper to taste. Transfer the mixture to a serving dish and keep hot.

4 Wipe the pan clean. Heat the oil and fry the eggs until just set. Serve the bubble and squeak on individual plates, adding a fried egg and two tomato halves to each portion. Sprinkle with black pepper.

Potato, Spinach and Pine Nut Gratin

Pine nuts add a satisfying crunch to this gratin of wafer-thin potato slices and spinach in a creamy cheese sauce.

Serves 2

INGREDIENTS
450 g/1 lb potatoes
1 garlic clove, crushed
3 spring onions, thinly sliced
150 ml/¼ pint/⅔ cup single cream
250 ml/8 fl oz/1 cup milk
225 g/8 oz frozen chopped
  spinach, thawed
115 g/4 oz Cheddar cheese, grated
25 g/1 oz/¼ cup pine nuts
salt and freshly ground black pepper

spinach

potatoes

garlic clove

pine nuts

Cheddar cheese

spring onions

single cream

1 Peel the potoates and cut them carefully into wafer-thin slices. Spread them out in a large, heavy-based, non-stick frying pan.

2 Scatter the crushed garlic and sliced spring onions evenly over the potatoes.

3 Pour the cream and milk over the potatoes. Place the pan over a gentle heat, cover and cook for 8 minutes or until the potatoes are tender.

4 Using both hands, squeeze the spinach dry. Add the spinach to the potatoes, mixing lightly. Cover the pan and cook for 2 minutes more.

5 Add salt and pepper to taste, then spoon the mixture into a gratin dish. Preheat the grill.

6 Sprinkle the grated cheese and pine nuts over the spinach mixture. Heat under the grill for 2–3 minutes until the topping is golden. A simple lettuce and tomato salad makes an excellent accompaniment to this dish.

Parmesan and Poached Egg Salad with Croûtons

Soft poached eggs, hot garlic croûtons and cool, crisp salad leaves make an unforgettable combination.

Serves 2

INGREDIENTS
½ small loaf white bread
75 ml/5 tbsp extra virgin olive oil
2 eggs
115 g/4 oz mixed salad leaves
2 garlic cloves, crushed
7.5 ml/½ tbsp white wine vinegar
25 g/1 oz Parmesan cheese

Parmesan cheese

mixed salad leaves

white bread

garlic cloves

eggs

1 Remove the crust from the bread. Cut the bread into 2.5 cm/1 in cubes.

2 Heat 30 ml/2 tbsp of the oil in a frying pan. Cook the bread for about 5 minutes, tossing the cubes occasionally, until they are golden brown.

3 Meanwhile, bring a pan of water to the boil. Carefully slide in the eggs, one at a time. Gently poach the eggs for 4 minutes until lightly cooked.

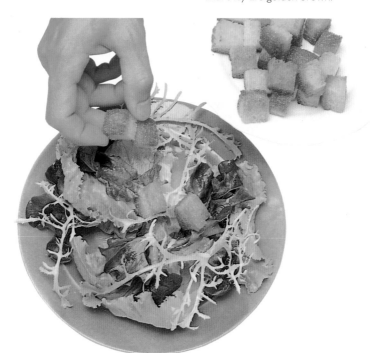

5 Heat the remaining oil in the pan, add the garlic and vinegar and cook over high heat for 1 minute. Pour the warm dressing over each salad.

4 Divide the salad leaves between two plates. Remove the croûtons from the pan and arrange them over the leaves. Wipe the pan clean with kitchen paper.

COOK'S TIP

Add a dash of vinegar to the water before poaching the eggs. This helps to keep the whites together. To ensure that a poached egg has a good shape, swirl the water with a spoon, whirlpool-fashion, before sliding in the egg.

6 Place a poached egg on each salad. Scatter with shavings of Parmesan and a little freshly ground black pepper, if liked.

Classic Greek Salad

If you have ever visited Greece you'll know that a Greek salad with a chunk of bread makes a delicious, filling meal.

Serves 4

INGREDIENTS
1 cos lettuce
$\frac{1}{2}$ cucumber, halved lengthways
4 tomatoes
8 spring onions
75 g/3 oz/2$\frac{1}{2}$ cups Greek
  black olives
115 g/4 oz feta cheese
90 ml/6 tbsp white wine vinegar
150 ml/$\frac{1}{4}$ pint/$\frac{2}{3}$ cup extra virgin
  olive oil
salt and freshly ground black pepper

cos lettuce

tomatoes

feta cheese

black olives

white wine vinegar

cucumber

spring onions

COOK'S TIP
The salad can be assembled in advance and chilled, but should only be dressed just before serving. Keep the dressing at room temperature as chilling deadens its flavour.

1 Tear the lettuce leaves into pieces and place them in a large mixing bowl. Slice the cucumber and add to the bowl.

2 Cut the tomatoes into wedges and put them into the bowl.

3 Slice the spring onions. Add them to the bowl with the olives and toss well.

4 Cut the feta cheese into cubes and add to the salad.

5 Put the vinegar, olive oil and seasoning into a small bowl and whisk well. Pour the dressing over the salad and toss to combine. Serve at once, with extra olives and chunks of bread, if liked.

Chicory, Fruit and Nut Salad

Mildly bitter chicory is wonderful with sweet fruit, and is especially delicious when complemented by a creamy curry sauce.

Serves 4

INGREDIENTS
45 ml/3 tbsp mayonnaise
15 ml/1 tbsp Greek yogurt
15 ml/1 tbsp mild curry paste
90 ml/6 tbsp single cream
$^1/_2$ iceberg lettuce
2 heads of chicory
50 g/2 oz/$^1/_2$ cup cashew nuts
50 g/2 oz/$1^1/_4$ cups flaked coconut
2 red apples
75 g/3 oz/$^1/_2$ cup currants

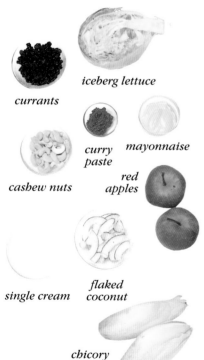

currants

iceberg lettuce

curry paste

mayonnaise

cashew nuts

red apples

single cream

flaked coconut

chicory

1 Mix the mayonnaise, Greek yogurt, curry paste and single cream in a small bowl. Cover and chill until required.

2 Tear the iceberg lettuce into pieces and put into a mixing bowl.

3 Cut the root end off each head of chicory, separate the leaves and add them to the lettuce. Preheat the grill.

4 Toast the cashew nuts for 2 minutes until golden. Tip into a bowl and set aside. Spread out the coconut flakes on a baking sheet. Grill for 1 minute until golden.

5 Quarter the apples and cut out the cores. Slice the apples and add to the lettuce with the coconut, cashew nuts and currants.

COOK'S TIP
Watch the coconut and cashew
nuts very carefully when grilling,
as they brown very fast.

6 Spoon the dressing over the salad,
toss lightly and serve.

Grilled Pepper Salad

Grilled peppers are delicious served hot with a sharp dressing. You can also serve them cold.

Serves 2

INGREDIENTS
1 red pepper
1 green pepper
1 yellow or orange pepper
1/2 radicchio, separated into leaves
1/2 frisée, separated into leaves
7.5 ml/1 1/2 tsp white wine vinegar
30 ml/2 tbsp extra virgin olive oil
175 g/6 oz goat's cheese
salt and freshly ground black pepper

frisée

red pepper

green pepper

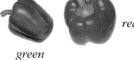

yellow pepper

goat's cheese

white wine vinegar

radicchio

1 Preheat the grill. Cut all the peppers in half. Cut each half into pieces.

2 Put the pepper pieces on a rack set over a grill pan. Grill for 10 minutes.

3 Meanwhile, divide the radicchio and frisée leaves between two plates. Chill until required.

4 Mix the vinegar and olive oil in a jar. Add salt and pepper to taste, close the jar tightly and shake well.

5 Slice the goat's cheese, place on a baking sheet and grill for 1 minute.

6 Arrange the peppers and grilled goat's cheese on the salads. Pour over the dressing and grind a little extra black pepper over each.

COOK'S TIP
Grill the peppers until they just start to blacken around the edges – don't let them burn.

Courgettes, Carrots and Pecans in Pitta Bread

Chunks of fried courgette served with a tangy salad in pitta pockets.

Serves 2

INGREDIENTS
2 carrots
25 g/1 oz/¹⁄₄ cup pecan nuts
4 spring onions, sliced
50 ml/2 fl oz/¹⁄₄ cup Greek yogurt
35 ml/7 tsp olive oil
5 ml/1 tsp lemon juice
15 ml/1 tbsp chopped fresh mint
2 courgettes
25 g/1 oz/¹⁄₄ cup plain flour
2 pitta breads
salt and freshly ground black pepper
shredded lettuce, to serve

courgettes

spring onions

pecan nuts   *lemon*

mint

Greek yogurt

carrots

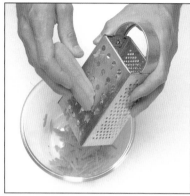

1 Top and tail the carrots. Grate them coarsely into a bowl.

2 Stir in the pecans and spring onions and toss well.

3 In a clean bowl, whisk the yogurt with 7.5 ml/1¹⁄₂ tsp of the olive oil, the lemon juice and the fresh mint. Stir the dressing into the carrot mixture and mix well. Cover and chill until required.

4 Top and tail the courgettes. Cut them diagonally into slices. Season the flour with salt and pepper. Spread it out on a plate and coat the courgette slices.

COOK'S TIP
Do not fill the pitta breads too soon or the carrot mixture will make the bread soggy.

5 Heat the remaining oil in a large frying pan. Add the coated courgette slices and cook for 3–4 minutes, turning once, until browned. Drain the courgettes on kitchen paper.

6 Make a slit in each pitta bread to form a pocket. Fill the pittas with the carrot mixture and the courgette slices. Serve on a bed of shredded lettuce.

Courgette Puffs with Salad and Balsamic Dressing

This unusual salad consists of deep-fried courgettes, flavoured with mint and served warm on a bed of salad leaves with a balsamic dressing.

Serves 2

INGREDIENTS
450 g/1 lb courgettes
75 g/3 oz/1½ cups fresh white
  breadcrumbs
1 egg
pinch of cayenne pepper
15 ml/1 tbsp chopped fresh mint
oil for deep-frying
15 ml/1 tbsp/3 tbsp balsamic vinegar
45 ml/3 tbsp extra virgin olive oil
200 g/7 oz mixed salad leaves
salt and freshly ground black pepper

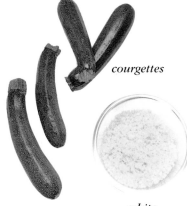

courgettes

*white
breadcrumbs*

*balsamic
vinegar*

*mixed salad
leaves*

egg   *mint*

1 Top and tail the courgettes. Coarsely grate them and put into a colander. Squeeze out the excess water, then put the courgettes into a bowl.

2 Add the breadcrumbs, egg, cayenne, mint and seasoning. Mix well.

3 Shape the courgette mixture into balls, about the size of walnuts.

4 Heat the oil for deep-frying to 180°C/350°F or until a cube of bread, when added to the oil, browns in 30–40 seconds. Deep-fry the courgette balls in batches for 2–3 minutes. Drain on kitchen paper.

5 Whisk the vinegar and oil together and season well.

6 Put the salad leaves in a bowl and pour over the dressing. Add the courgette puffs and toss lightly together. Serve at once, while the courgette puffs are still crisp.

Vegetable and Satay Salad

Baby new potatoes, tender vegetables and crunchy chick-peas are smothered in a creamy peanut dressing.

Serves 4

INGREDIENTS

450 g/1 lb baby new potatoes
1 small head cauliflower, broken
  into small florets
225 g/8 oz French beans, trimmed
400 g/14 oz can chick-peas, drained
115 g/4 oz watercress sprigs
115 g/4 oz beansprouts
8 spring onions, sliced
60 ml/4 tbsp crunchy peanut butter
150 ml/¹/₄ pint/²/₃ cup hot water
5 ml/1 tsp chilli sauce
10 ml/2 tsp soft brown sugar
5 ml/1 tsp soy sauce
5 ml/1 tsp lime juice

cauliflower

watercress

soy sauce

spring onions

crunchy peanut butter

soft brown sugar

chick-peas

beansprouts

chilli sauce

French beans

lime

baby new potatoes

1 Put the potatoes into a pan and add water to just cover. Bring to the boil and cook for 10–12 minutes or until the potatoes are just tender when pierced with the point of a sharp knife. Drain and refresh under cold running water. Drain once again.

2 Meanwhile, bring another pan of salted water to the boil. Add the cauliflower and cook for 5 minutes, then add the beans and cook for 5 minutes more. Drain both vegetables, refresh under cold water and drain again.

3 Put the cauliflower and beans into a large bowl and add the chick-peas. Halve the potatoes and add. Toss lightly. Mix the watercress, beansprouts and spring onions together. Divide between four plates and pile the vegetables on top.

4 Put the peanut butter into a bowl and stir in the water. Add the chilli sauce, brown sugar, soy sauce and lime juice. Whisk well then drizzle the dressing over the vegetables.

Fresh Spinach and Avocado Salad

Young tender spinach leaves make a change from lettuce and are delicious served with avocado, cherry tomatoes and radishes in a tofu sauce.

Serves 2-3

INGREDIENTS
1 large avocado
juice of 1 lime
225 g/8 oz fresh baby spinach leaves
115 g/4 oz cherry tomatoes
4 spring onions, sliced
½ cucumber
50 g/2 oz radishes, sliced

FOR THE DRESSING
115 g/4 oz soft silken tofu
45 ml/3 tbsp milk
10 ml/2 tsp mustard
2.5 ml/½ tsp white wine vinegar
pinch of cayenne
salt and freshly ground black pepper

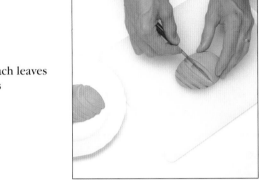
tofu *spring onions* *spinach leaves*
cherry tomatoes
avocado
white wine vinegar
mustard
cayenne *lime*
cucumber
radishes
milk

1 Cut the avocado in half, remove the stone and strip off the skin. Cut the flesh into slices. Transfer to a plate, drizzle over the lime juice and set aside.

2 Wash and dry the spinach leaves. Put them in a mixing bowl.

COOK'S TIP
Use soft silken tofu rather than the firm block variety. It can be found in most supermarkets in long-life cartons.

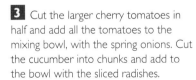
3 Cut the larger cherry tomatoes in half and add all the tomatoes to the mixing bowl, with the spring onions. Cut the cucumber into chunks and add to the bowl with the sliced radishes.

4 Make the dressing. Put the tofu, milk, mustard, wine vinegar and cayenne in a food processor or blender. Add salt and pepper to taste. Process for 30 seconds until smooth. Scrape the dressing into a bowl and add a little extra milk if you like a thinner dressing. Sprinkle with a little extra cayenne and garnish with radish roses and herb sprigs, if liked.

New Spring Salad

This chunky salad makes a satisfying meal, use other spring vegetables, if you like.

Serves 4

INGREDIENTS
675 g/1½ lb small new
  potatoes, halved
400 g/14 oz can broad
  beans, drained
115 g/4 oz cherry tomatoes
50 g/2 oz/2½ cups walnut halves
30 ml/2 tbsp white wine vinegar
15 ml/1 tbsp wholegrain mustard
60 ml/4 tbsp olive oil
pinch of sugar
225 g/8 oz young asparagus
  spears, trimmed
6 spring onions, trimmed
salt and freshly ground black pepper
baby spinach leaves, to serve

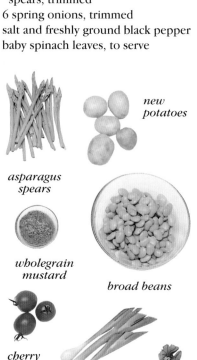

new
potatoes

asparagus
spears

wholegrain
mustard

broad beans

cherry
tomatoes

spring
onions

walnut halves

1 Put the potatoes in a pan. Cover with cold water and bring to the boil. Cook for 10 –12 minutes, until tender. Meanwhile, tip the broad beans into a bowl. Cut the tomatoes in half and add them to the bowl with the walnuts.

2 Put the white wine vinegar, mustard, olive oil and sugar into a jar. Add salt and pepper to taste. Close the jar tightly and shake well.

3 Add the asparagus to the potatoes and cook for 3 minutes more. Drain the cooked vegetables well, cool under cold running water and drain again. Thickly slice the potatoes. Cut the spring onions into halves.

4 Add the asparagus, potatoes and spring onions to the bowl containing the broad bean mixture. Pour the dressing over the salad and toss well. Serve on a bed of baby spinach leaves.

Potato Salad with Egg and Lemon Dressing

Potato salads are a popular addition to any salad spread and are enjoyed with an assortment of cold meats and fish. This recipe draws on the contrasting flavours of egg and lemon. Chopped parsley provides a fresh finish.

Serves 4

INGREDIENTS

900 g/2 lb new potatoes, scrubbed or scraped
salt and pepper
1 medium onion, finely chopped
1 egg, hard-boiled
300 ml/10 fl oz/1¼ cups mayonnaise
1 clove garlic, crushed
finely grated zest and juice of 1 lemon
60 ml/4 tbsp chopped fresh parsley

COOK'S TIP

At certain times of the year potatoes are inclined to fall apart when boiled. This usually coincides with the end of a particular season when potatoes become starchy. Early-season varieties are therefore best for making salads.

egg

garlic

onion

lemon

new potatoes

1 Bring the potatoes to the boil in a saucepan of salted water. Simmer for 20 minutes. Drain and allow to cool. Cut the potatoes into large dice, season well and combine with the onion.

2 Shell the hard-boiled egg and grate into a mixing bowl, then add the mayonnaise. Combine the garlic and lemon zest and juice in a small bowl and stir into the mayonnaise.

3 Fold in the chopped parsley, mix thoroughly into the potatoes and serve.

Soft Leeks with Parsley, Egg and Walnut Dressing

In French cooking leeks are valued for their smooth texture as well as for their flavour. Here they are served as a *salade tiède* (warm salad), with an earthy-rich sauce of parsley, egg and walnut. It is an ideal dish to serve with pâté and boiled new potatoes for a gourmet picnic feast.

Serves 4

INGREDIENTS
700 g/1½ lb young leeks
1 egg

DRESSING
25 g/1 oz fresh parsley
30 ml/2 tbsp olive oil, preferably French
juice of ½ lemon
50 g/2 oz/½ cup broken walnuts, toasted
5 ml/1 tsp caster (superfine) sugar
salt and pepper

parsley

walnuts

leeks

egg

1 Bring a saucepan of salted water to the boil. Cut the leeks into 10 cm/4 in lengths and rinse well to flush out any grit or soil. Cook the leeks for 8 minutes. Drain and part-cool under running water.

2 Lower the egg into boiling water and cook for 12 minutes. Cool under running water, shell and set aside.

3 For the dressing, finely chop the parsley in a food processor.

4 Add the olive oil, lemon juice and toasted walnuts. Blend for 1–2 minutes until smooth.

5 Adjust the consistency with about 90 ml/6 tbsp/⅓ cup water. Add the sugar and season to taste with salt and pepper.

6 Place the leeks on an attractive plate, then spoon on the sauce. Finely grate the hard-boiled egg and scatter over the sauce. Serve at room temperature.

Deep-fried Courgettes with Chilli Sauce

Crunchy coated courgettes are great served with a fiery tomato sauce.

Serves 2

INGREDIENTS
15 ml/1 tbsp olive oil
1 onion, finely chopped
1 red chilli, seeded and finely diced
10 ml/2 tsp hot chilli powder
400 g/14 oz can chopped tomatoes
1 vegetable stock cube
50 ml/2 fl oz/¼ cup hot water
450 g/1 lb courgettes
150 ml/¼ pint/⅔ cup milk
50 g/2 oz/½ cup plain flour
oil for deep-frying
salt and freshly ground black pepper
thyme sprigs, to garnish

TO SERVE
lettuce leaves
watercress sprigs
slices of seeded bread

courgettes

chopped tomatoes

onion

red chilli

plain flour

stock cube

milk

chilli powder

1 Heat the oil in a pan. Add the onion and cook for 2–3 minutes. Add the chilli. Stir in the chilli powder and cook for 30 seconds.

2 Add the tomatoes. Crumble in the stock cube and stir in the water. Cover and cook for 10 minutes.

3 Meanwhile, top and tail the courgettes. Cut into 5 mm/¼ in slices.

4 Pour the milk into one shallow dish and spread out the flour in another. Dip the courgettes first in the milk, then into the flour, until well-coated.

5 Heat the oil for deep-frying to 180°C/350°F or until a cube of bread, when added to the oil, browns in 30–45 seconds. Add the courgettes in batches and deep-fry for 3–4 minutes until crisp. Drain on kitchen paper.

6 Place two or three lettuce leaves on each serving plate. Add a few sprigs of watercress and fan out the bread slices to one side. Season the sauce, spoon some on to each plate, top with the crisp courgettes and garnish with the thyme sprigs. Serve at once with salad and bread.

Cumin-spiced Marrow and Spinach

Tender chunks of marrow with spinach in a creamy, cumin-flavoured sauce.

Serves 2

INGREDIENTS
1/2 marrow, about 450 g/1 lb
30 ml/2 tbsp vegetable oil
10 ml/2 tsp cumin seeds
1 small red chilli, seeded and
   finely chopped
30 ml/2 tbsp water
50 g/2 oz tender young
   spinach leaves
90 ml/6 tbsp single cream
salt and freshly ground black pepper

spinach leaves

cumin seeds

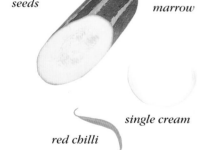

marrow

single cream

red chilli

1 Peel the marrow and cut it in half. Scoop out the seeds. Cut the flesh into cubes.

2 Heat the oil in a large frying pan. Add the cumin seeds and the chopped chilli. Cook for 1 minute.

3 Add the marrow and water to the pan. Cover with foil or a lid and simmer for 8 minutes, stirring occasionally, until the marrow is just tender. Remove the cover and cook for 2 minutes more or until most of the water has evaporated.

4 Put the spinach leaves in a colander. Rinse well under cold water, drain and pat dry with kitchen paper. Tear into rough pieces.

5 Add the spinach to the marrow, replace the cover and cook gently for 1 minute. Serve hot.

COOK'S TIP

Be careful when handling chillies as the juice can burn sensitive skin. Wear rubber gloves or wash hands thoroughly after preparation.

6 Stir in the cream and cook over a high heat for 2 minutes. Add salt and pepper to taste, and serve. An Indian rice dish would be a good accompaniment. Alternatively, serve with naan bread.

Chilli Beans with Basmati Rice

Red kidney beans, tomatoes and chilli make a great combination. Serve with pasta or pitta bread instead of rice, if you prefer.

Serves 4

INGREDIENTS
350 g/12 oz/2 cups basmati rice
30 ml/2 tbsp olive oil
1 large onion, chopped
1 garlic clove, crushed
15 ml/1 tbsp hot chilli powder
15 ml/1 tbsp plain flour
15 ml/1 tbsp tomato purée
400 g/14 oz can chopped tomatoes
400 g/14 oz can red kidney
  beans, drained
150 ml/¼ pint/⅔ cup hot
  vegetable stock
chopped fresh parsley, to garnish
salt and freshly ground black pepper

basmati rice

chopped tomatoes

chilli powder

onion   tomato purée

garlic clove

stock cube   red kidney beans   plain flour

1 Wash the rice several times under cold running water. Drain well. Bring a large pan of water to the boil. Add the rice and cook for 10–12 minutes, until tender. Meanwhile, heat the oil in a frying pan. Add the onion and garlic and cook for 2 minutes.

2 Stir the chilli powder and flour into the onion and garlic mixture. Cook for 2 minutes, stirring frequently.

3 Stir in the tomato purée and chopped tomatoes. Rinse the kidney beans under cold water, drain well and add to the pan with the hot vegetable stock. Cover and cook for 12 minutes, stirring occasionally.

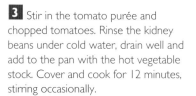

4 Season the chilli sauce with salt and pepper. Drain the rice and serve at once, with the chilli beans, sprinkled with a little chopped fresh parsley.

Spicy Cauliflower and Potato Salad

A delicious cold vegetable salad with a hot spicy dressing.

Serves 2–3

INGREDIENTS
1 medium cauliflower
2 medium potatoes
7.5 ml/1½ tsp caraway seeds
5 ml/1 tsp ground coriander
2.5 ml/½ tsp hot chilli powder
juice of 1 lemon
60 ml/4 tbsp olive oil
salt and freshly ground black pepper

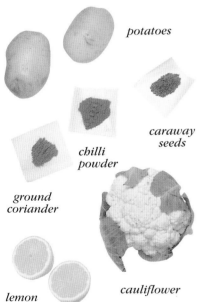

potatoes

chilli powder

caraway seeds

ground coriander

lemon

cauliflower

1 Break the cauliflower into small florets. Peel the potatoes and cut them into chunks.

2 Bring a large pan of water to the boil. Add the cauliflower florets and potato chunks and cook for 8 minutes until just tender.

3 Meanwhile, heat a non-stick frying pan. Add the caraway seeds and fry, shaking the pan constantly, for 1 minute. Tip the roasted seeds into a bowl and add the ground coriander and chilli powder, with salt and pepper to taste. Stir in the lemon juice and olive oil and mix to a paste.

4 Drain the vegetables well. Add them to the bowl and toss to coat in the chilli dressing. Serve at once, with hot pitta bread or brown rice.

Bengali-style Vegetables

A hot dry curry using spices that do not require long slow cooking.

Serves 4

INGREDIENTS

½ medium cauliflower, broken into
  small florets
1 large potato, peeled and cut into
  2.5 cm/1 in dice
115 g/4 oz French beans, trimmed
2 courgettes, halved lengthways
  and sliced
2 green chillies
2.5 cm/1 in piece of fresh root
  ginger, peeled
120 ml/4 fl oz/½ cup natural yogurt
10 ml/2 tsp ground coriander
2.5 ml/½ tsp ground turmeric
25 g/1 oz/2 tbsp ghee
2.5 ml/½ tsp garam masala
5 ml/1 tsp cumin seeds
10 ml/2 tsp sugar
pinch each of ground cloves,
  ground cinnamon and
    ground cardamom
salt and freshly ground black pepper

1 Bring a large pan of water to the boil. Add the cauliflower and potato and cook for 5 minutes. Add the beans and courgettes and cook for 2–3 minutes.

2 Meanwhile, cut the chillies in half, remove the seeds and roughly chop the flesh. Finely chop the ginger. Mix the chillies and ginger in a small bowl.

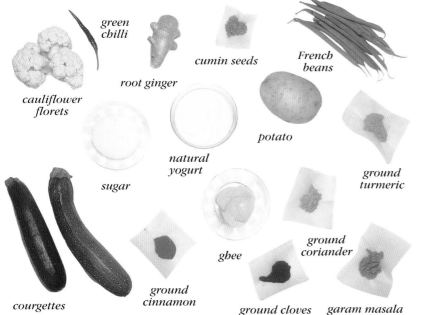

green chilli

cumin seeds

French beans

root ginger

cauliflower florets

potato

natural yogurt

sugar

ground turmeric

courgettes

ghee

ground cinnamon

ground coriander

ground cloves

garam masala

3 Drain the vegetables and tip them into a bowl. Add the chilli and ginger mixture, with the yogurt, ground coriander and turmeric. Season with plenty of salt and pepper and mix well.

4 Heat the ghee in a large frying pan. Add the vegetable mixture and cook over a high heat for 2 minutes, stirring from time to time.

138

5 Stir in the garam masala and cumin seeds and cook for 2 minutes.

6 Stir in the sugar and remaining spices and cook for 1 minute or until all the liquid has evaporated.

COOK'S TIP

If ghee is not available you can clarify your own butter. Melt 50 g/2 oz/¼ cup butter slowly in a small pan. Remove from the heat and leave for about 5 minutes. Pour off the clear yellow clarified butter, leaving the sediment in the pan.

Vegetable Fajita

A colourful medley of mushrooms and peppers in a spicy sauce, wrapped in tortillas and served with creamy guacamole.

Serves 2

INGREDIENTS
1 onion
1 red pepper
1 green pepper
1 yellow pepper
1 garlic clove, crushed
225 g/8 oz mushrooms
90 ml/6 tbsp vegetable oil
30 ml/2 tbsp medium chilli powder
salt and freshly ground black pepper
coriander sprigs and 1 lime, cut into
  wedges, to garnish

FOR THE GUACAMOLE
1 ripe avocado
1 shallot, roughly chopped
1 green chilli, seeded and
  roughly chopped
juice of 1 lime

TO SERVE
4–6 flour tortillas, warmed

green pepper yellow pepper red pepper

mushrooms

green chilli

garlic clove

shallot

avocado

lime chilli powder onion

1 Slice the onion. Cut the peppers in half, remove the seeds and cut the flesh into strips. Combine the onion and peppers in a bowl. Add the crushed garlic and mix lightly.

2 Remove the mushroom stalks. Save for making stock, or discard. Slice the mushroom caps and add to the pepper mixture in the bowl. Mix the oil and chilli powder in a cup, pour over the vegetable mixture and stir well. Set aside.

3 Make the guacamole. Cut the avocado in half and remove the stone and the peel. Put the flesh into a food processor or blender with the shallot, green chilli and lime juice. Process for 1 minute until smooth. Scrape into a small bowl, cover closely and put in the fridge to chill until required.

4 Heat a frying pan or wok until very hot. Add the marinated vegetables and stir-fry over high heat for 5–6 minutes until the mushrooms and pepper are just tender. Season well. Spoon a little of the filling on to each tortilla and roll up. Garnish with fresh coriander and lime wedges and serve with the guacamole.

Curried Eggs

Hard-boiled eggs are served on a bed of mild creamy sauce with a hint of curry.

Serves 2

INGREDIENTS

4 eggs
15 ml/1 tbsp sunflower oil
1 small onion, finely chopped
2.5 cm/1 in piece of fresh root
  ginger, peeled and grated
2.5 ml/½ tsp ground cumin
2.5 ml/½ tsp garam masala
25 ml/1½ tbsp tomato purée
10 ml/2 tsp tandoori paste
10 ml/2 tsp lemon juice
50 ml/2 fl oz/¼ cup single cream
15 ml/1 tbsp chopped
  fresh coriander
salt and freshly ground black pepper
coriander sprigs, to garnish

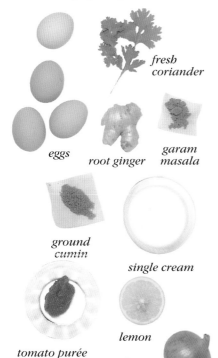

fresh coriander

eggs   *root ginger*   *garam masala*

ground cumin

single cream

tomato purée

lemon

tandoori paste

onion

1 Put the eggs in a pan of water. Bring to the boil, lower the heat and simmer for 10 minutes.

2 Meanwhile, heat the oil in a frying pan. Cook the onion for 2–3 minutes. Add the ginger and cook for 1 minute.

3 Stir in the ground cumin, garam masala, tomato purée, tandoori paste, lemon juice and cream. Cook for 1–2 minutes, then stir in the coriander. Add salt and pepper to taste.

4 Drain the eggs, remove the shells and cut each egg in half. Spoon the sauce into a serving bowl, top with the eggs and garnish with the fresh coriander. Serve at once.

Breaded Aubergine with Hot Vinaigrette

Crisp on the outside, beautifully tender within, these aubergine slices taste wonderful with a spicy dressing flavoured with chilli and capers.

Serves 2

INGREDIENTS
1 large aubergine
50 g/2 oz/¹/₂ cup plain flour
2 eggs, beaten
115 g/4 oz/2 cups fresh
  white breadcrumbs
vegetable oil for frying
1 head radicchio
salt and freshly ground black pepper

FOR THE DRESSING
30 ml/2 tbsp olive oil
1 garlic clove, crushed
15 ml/1 tbsp capers, drained
15 ml/1 tbsp white wine vinegar
15 ml/1 tbsp chilli oil

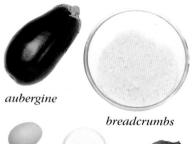

aubergine

breadcrumbs

eggs

plain flour

radicchio

capers

white wine vinegar

garlic clove

COOK'S TIP
When serving a salad with a warm dressing use robust leaves that will stand up to the heat.

1 Top and tail the aubergine. Cut it into 5 mm/¹/₄ in slices. Set aside.

2 Season the flour with a generous amount of salt and black pepper. Spread out in a shallow dish. Pour the beaten eggs into a second dish, and spread out the breadcrumbs in a third.

3 Dip the aubergine slices in the flour, then in the beaten egg and finally in the breadcrumbs, patting them on to make an even coating.

4 Pour vegetable oil into a large frying pan to a depth of about 5 mm/¹/₄ in. Heat the oil, then fry the aubergine slices for 3–4 minutes, turning once. Drain on kitchen paper.

5 Heat the olive oil in a small pan. Add the garlic and the capers and cook over gentle heat for 1 minute. Increase the heat, add the vinegar and cook for 30 seconds. Stir in the chilli oil and remove the pan from the heat.

6 Arrange the radicchio leaves on two plates. Top with the hot aubergine slices. Drizzle over the vinaigrette and serve.

Creamy Cannellini Beans with Asparagus

Cannellini beans in a creamy sauce contrast with tender asparagus in this tasty toast topper.

Serves 2

INGREDIENTS

10 ml/2 tsp butter
1 small onion, finely chopped
1 small carrot, grated
5 ml/1 tsp fresh thyme leaves
400 g/14 oz can cannellini
  beans, drained
150 ml/¹/₄ pint/²/₃ cup single cream
115 g/4 oz young asparagus
  spears, trimmed
2 slices of fresh cut Granary bread
salt and freshly ground black pepper

Granary bread *carrot* *thyme*

single cream *butter* *asparagus spears*

onion *cannellini beans*

parsley

1 Melt the butter in a pan. Add the onion and carrot and fry over a moderate heat for 4 minutes until soft. Add the thyme leaves.

2 Rinse the cannellini beans under cold running water. Drain thoroughly, then add to the onion and carrot. Mix lightly.

3 Pour in the cream and heat slowly to just below boiling point, stirring occasionally. Remove the pan from the heat and add salt and pepper to taste. Preheat the grill.

4 Place the asparagus spears in a saucepan. Pour over just enough boiling water to cover. Poach for 3–4 minutes until the spears are just tender.

5 Meanwhile, toast the bread under the grill until both sides are golden.

6 Place the toast on individual plates. Drain the asparagus and divide the spears between the slices of toast. Spoon the bean mixture over each portion and serve.

COOK'S TIP
Use your favourite variety of canned beans such as borlotti, haricot or flageolets.

Red Fried Rice

This vibrant rice dish owes its appeal as much to the bright colours of red onion, red pepper and cherry tomatoes as it does to their distinctive flavours.

Serves 2

INGREDIENTS
115 g/4 oz/³⁄₄ cup basmati rice
30 ml/2 tbsp groundnut oil
1 small red onion, chopped
1 red pepper, seeded and chopped
225 g/8 oz cherry tomatoes, halved
2 eggs, beaten
salt and freshly ground black pepper

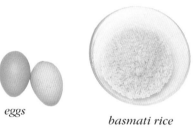

eggs

basmati rice

cherry tomatoes

red onion

red pepper

1 Wash the rice several times under cold running water. Drain well. Bring a large pan of water to the boil, add the rice and cook for 10–12 minutes.

2 Meanwhile, heat the oil in a wok until very hot. Add the onion and red pepper and stir-fry for 2–3 minutes. Add the cherry tomatoes and stir-fry for a further 2 minutes.

3 Pour in the beaten eggs all at once. Cook for 30 seconds without stirring, then stir to break up the egg as it sets.

4 Drain the cooked rice thoroughly, add to the wok and toss it over the heat with the vegetable and egg mixture for 3 minutes. Season the fried rice with salt and pepper to taste.

Chick-pea Stew

This hearty chick-pea and vegetable stew makes a filling meal. It is delicious served with garlic-flavoured mashed potato.

Serves 4

INGREDIENTS

30 ml/2 tbsp olive oil
1 small onion, chopped
225 g/8 oz carrots, halved
  and thinly sliced
2.5 ml/½ tsp ground cumin
5 ml/1 tsp ground coriander
30 ml/2 tbsp plain flour
225 g/8 oz courgettes, sliced
200 g/7 oz can sweetcorn, drained
400 g/14 oz can chick-peas, drained
30 ml/2 tbsp tomato purée
200 ml/7 fl oz/scant 1 cup hot
  vegetable stock
salt and freshly ground black pepper

onion   *tomato purée*

sweetcorn   *chick-peas*

stock cube

ground cumin

ground coriander

plain flour

courgettes

carrots

1 Heat the oil in a frying pan. Add the onion and carrots. Toss to coat the vegetables in the oil, then cook over moderate heat for 4 minutes.

2 Add the ground cumin, coriander and flour. Stir and cook for 1 minute.

COOK'S TIP

For speedy garlic-flavoured mashed potatoes simply mash potatoes with garlic butter and stir in chopped fresh parsley and a little crème fraîche.

3 Cut the courgette slices in half. Add them to the pan with the sweetcorn, chick-peas, tomato purée and vegetable stock. Stir well. Cook for 10 minutes, stirring frequently.

4 Taste the stew and add salt and pepper. Serve at once, with garlic-flavoured mashed potato (see Cook's Tip), if liked.

Aubergine Pilaff

This hearty dish is made with bulgur wheat and aubergine, flavoured with fresh mint.

Serves 2

INGREDIENTS
2 medium aubergines
60-90 ml/4-6 tbsp sunflower oil
1 small onion, finely chopped
175 g/6 oz/1 cup bulgur wheat
450 ml/16 fl oz/scant 2 cups
  vegetable stock
30 ml/2 tbsp pine nuts, toasted
15 ml/1 tbsp chopped fresh mint
salt and freshly ground black pepper

FOR THE GARNISH
lime wedges
lemon wedges
torn mint leaves

mint

pine nuts

stock cube

onion

bulgur wheat

aubergines

1 Trim the ends from the aubergines. Using a sharp knife, cut them into neat sticks and then into 1 cm/½ in dice.

COOK'S TIP

To cut down on the cooking time, soak the bulgur wheat in water to cover by 2.5 cm/1 in for up to 8 hours. Drain and continue as described in the recipe, reducing the cooking time to 8 minutes.

2 Heat 60 ml/4 tbsp of the oil in a large frying pan. Add the onion and sauté for 1 minute.

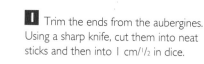

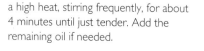

3 Add the diced aubergine. Cook over a high heat, stirring frequently, for about 4 minutes until just tender. Add the remaining oil if needed.

4 Stir in the bulgur wheat, mixing well, then pour in the vegetable stock. Bring to the boil, then lower the heat and simmer for 10 minutes or until all the liquid has evaporated. Season to taste.

5 Add the pine nuts, stir gently with a wooden spoon, then stir in the mint.

6 Spoon the pilaff on to individual plates and garnish each portion with lime and lemon wedges. Sprinkle with torn mint leaves for extra colour.

Houmus with Pan-fried Courgettes

Pan-fried courgettes are perfect for dipping into home-made houmus.

Serves 4

INGREDIENTS
225 g/8 oz can chick-peas
2 garlic cloves, roughly chopped
90 ml/6 tbsp lemon juice
60 ml/4 tbsp tahini paste
75 ml/5 tbsp olive oil, plus extra
  to serve
5 ml/1 tsp ground cumin
450 g/1 lb small courgettes
salt and freshly ground black pepper

TO SERVE
paprika
pitta bread
black olives

courgettes

chick-peas

lemon

tahini paste

garlic cloves

ground cumin

1 Drain the chick-peas, reserving the liquid from the can, and tip them into a food processor or blender. Blend to a smooth purée, adding a small amount of the reserved liquid if necessary.

2 Mix the garlic, lemon juice and tahini together and add to the food processor or blender. Process until smooth. With the machine running, gradually add 45 ml/3 tbsp of the olive oil through the feeder tube or lid.

3 Add the cumin, with salt and pepper to taste. Process to mix, then scrape the houmus into a bowl. Cover and chill until required.

4 Top and tail the courgettes. Slice them lengthways into even-size pieces.

5 Heat the remaining oil in a large frying pan. Season the courgettes and fry them for 2–3 minutes on each side until just tender.

COOK'S TIP
Houmus is also delicious served with pan-fried or grilled aubergine slices.

6 Divide the courgettes among four individual plates. Spoon a portion of houmus on to each plate, sprinkle with paprika, add two or three pieces of sliced pitta bread and serve with olives.

Lentil Stir-fry

Mushrooms, artichokes, sugar snap peas and lentils make a satisfying stir-fry supper.

Serves 2–3

INGREDIENTS

115 g/4 oz sugar snap peas
25 g/1 oz butter
1 small onion, chopped
115 g/4 oz cup or brown cap
  mushrooms, sliced
400 g/14 oz can artichoke hearts,
  drained and halved
400 g/14 oz can green
  lentils, drained
60 ml/4 tbsp single cream
25 g/1 oz/¼ cup flaked
  almonds, toasted
salt and freshly ground black pepper
French bread, to serve

single cream

green lentils

cup mushrooms

sugar snap peas

flaked almonds

artichoke hearts

onion

COOK'S TIP
Use Greek yogurt instead of the cream, if preferred.

1 Bring a pan of salted water to the boil, add the sugar snap peas and cook for about 4 minutes until just tender. Drain, refresh under cold running water, then drain again. Pat dry the peas with kitchen paper and set aside.

2 Melt the butter in a frying pan. Cook the chopped onion for 2–3 minutes, stirring occasionally.

3 Add the sliced mushrooms to the onion. Stir until combined, then cook for 2–3 minutes until just tender. Add the artichokes, sugar snap peas and lentils to the pan. Stir-fry for 2 minutes.

4 Stir in the cream and almonds and cook for 1 minute. Season to taste. Serve at once, with chunks of French bread.

Nut Pilaff with Omelette Rolls

A wonderful mixture of textures – soft fluffy rice with crunchy nuts and omelette rolls.

Serves 2

INGREDIENTS

175 g/6 oz/1 cup basmati rice
15 ml/1 tbsp sunflower oil
1 small onion, chopped
1 red pepper, finely diced
350 ml/12 fl oz/1½ cups hot
  vegetable stock
2 eggs
25 g/1 oz/¼ cup salted peanuts
15 ml/1 tbsp soy sauce
salt and freshly ground black pepper
parsley sprigs, to garnish

salted peanuts *parsley* *onion*

stock cube *eggs* *red pepper*

basmati rice *soy sauce*

1 Wash the rice several times under cold running water. Drain thoroughly. Heat half the oil in a large frying pan. Fry the onion and pepper for 2–3 minutes then stir in the rice and stock. Bring to the boil and cook for 10 minutes until the rice is tender.

2 Meanwhile, beat the eggs lightly with salt and pepper to taste. Heat the remaining oil in a second large frying pan. Pour in the eggs and tilt the pan to cover the base thinly. Cook the omelette for 1 minute, then flip it over and cook the other side for 1 minute.

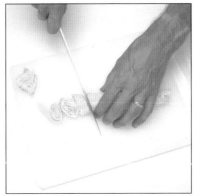

3 Slide the omelette on to a clean board and roll it up tightly. Cut the omelette roll into 8 slices.

4 Stir the peanuts and the soy sauce into the pilaff and add black pepper to taste. Turn the pilaff into a serving dish, arrange the omelette rolls on top and garnish with the parsley. Serve at once.

Kedgeree with French Beans and Mushrooms

Crunchy French beans and mushrooms are the star ingredients in this vegetarian version of an old favourite.

Serves 2

INGREDIENTS

115 g/4 oz/³/₄ cup basmati rice
3 eggs
175 g/6 oz French beans, trimmed
50 g/2 oz/¹/₄ cup butter
1 onion, finely chopped
225 g/8 oz brown cap mushrooms, quartered
30 ml/2 tbsp single cream
15 ml/1 tbsp chopped fresh parsley
salt and freshly ground black pepper

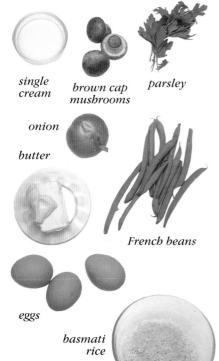

single cream *brown cap mushrooms* *parsley*

onion

butter

French beans

eggs

basmati rice

1 Wash the rice several times under cold running water. Drain thoroughly. Bring a pan of water to the boil, add the rice and cook for 10–12 minutes until tender. Drain thoroughly.

2 Half fill a second pan with water, add the eggs and bring to the boil. Lower the heat and simmer for 8 minutes. Drain the eggs, cool them under cold water, then remove the shells.

3 Bring another pan of water to the boil and cook the French beans for 5 minutes. Drain, refresh under cold running water, then drain again.

4 Melt the butter in a large frying pan. Add the onion and mushrooms. Cook for 2–3 minutes over a moderate heat.

5 Add the French beans and rice to the onion mixture. Stir lightly to mix. Cook for 2 minutes. Cut the hard-boiled eggs in wedges and add them to the pan.

6 Stir in the cream and parsley, taking care not to break up the eggs. Reheat the kedgeree, but do not allow it to boil. Serve at once.

Chick-pea Falafel with Coriander Dip

Little balls of spicy chick-pea purée, deep-fried until crisp, are served together with a coriander-flavoured mayonnaise.

Serves 4

INGREDIENTS
400 g/14 oz can chick-peas, drained
6 spring onions, finely sliced
1 egg
2.5 ml/½ tsp ground turmeric
1 garlic clove, crushed
5 ml/1 tsp ground cumin
60 ml/4 tbsp chopped
  fresh coriander
oil for deep-frying
1 small red chilli, seeded and
  finely chopped
45 ml/3 tbsp mayonnaise
salt and freshly ground black pepper
coriander sprig, to garnish

spring onions chick-peas coriander
ground turmeric
ground cumin
egg garlic clove red chilli
mayonnaise

COOK'S TIP
If you have time, chill the chick-pea purée before making it into balls. It will be easier to shape.

1 Tip the chick-peas into a food processor or blender. Add the spring onions and process to a smooth purée. Add the egg, turmeric, garlic, cumin and 15 ml/1 tbsp of the chopped coriander. Process briefly to mix, then add salt and pepper to taste.

2 Working with clean wet hands, shape the chick-pea mixture into about 16 small balls.

3 Heat the oil for deep-frying to 180°C/350°F or until a cube of bread, when added to the oil, browns in 30–45 seconds. Deep-fry the falafel in batches for 2–3 minutes or until golden. Drain on kitchen paper, then place in a serving bowl.

4 Stir the remaining coriander and the chilli into the mayonnaise. Garnish with the coriander sprig and serve alongside the falafel.

Three Bean Salad with Yogurt Dressing

This tangy bean and pasta salad is great on its own or can be served as a side dish.

Serves 3–4

INGREDIENTS

75 g/3 oz penne or other dried
  pasta shapes
2 tomatoes
200 g/7 oz can red kidney
  beans, drained
200 g/7 oz can cannellini
  beans, drained
200 g/7 oz can chick-peas, drained
1 green pepper, seeded and diced
75 ml/3 tbsp natural yogurt
30 ml/2 tbsp sunflower oil
grated rind of ¹/₂ lemon
10 ml/2 tsp wholegrain mustard
5 ml/1 tsp chopped fresh oregano
salt and freshly ground black pepper

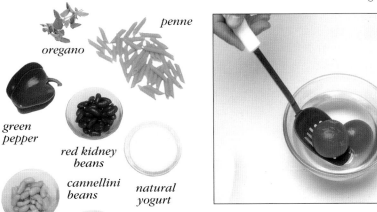

oregano *penne*

green pepper *red kidney beans* *cannellini beans* *natural yogurt* *chick-peas*

lemon *wholegrain mustard* *tomatoes*

1 Bring a large pan of salted water to the boil. Add the pasta and cook for 10–12 minutes until just tender. Drain, cool under cold water and drain again.

2 Make a cross with the tip of a sharp knife in each of the tomatoes. Plunge them into a bowl of boiling water for 30 seconds. Remove with a slotted spoon or spatula, run under cold water and peel away the skins. Cut the tomatoes into segments.

3 Drain the canned beans and chick-peas in a colander, rinse them under cold water and drain again. Tip into a bowl. Add the tomato segments, green pepper and pasta.

4 Whisk the yogurt until smooth. Gradually whisk in the oil, lemon rind and mustard. Stir in the oregano and salt and pepper to taste. Pour the dressing over the salad and toss well.

Pumpkin and Pistachio Risotto

This elegant combination of creamy golden rice and orange pumpkin can be as pale or bright as you like by adding different quantities of saffron.

Serves 4

INGREDIENTS

1.1 litres/2 pints/5 cups vegetable
   stock or water
generous pinch of saffron threads
30 ml/2 tbsp olive oil
1 medium onion, chopped
2 garlic cloves, crushed
450 g/1 lb arborio rice
900 g/2 lb pumpkin, peeled, seeded
   and cut into 2 cm/¾ in cubes
200 ml/7 fl oz/¾ cup dry white wine
15 g/½ oz Parmesan cheese, finely
   grated
50 g/2 oz/½ cup pistachios
45 ml/3 tbsp chopped fresh marjoram
   or oregano, plus extra leaves, to
   garnish
salt, freshly grated nutmeg and ground
   black pepper

1 Bring the stock or water to the boil and reduce to a low simmer. Ladle a little stock into a small bowl. Add the saffron threads and leave to infuse.

4 Gradually add the stock or water, a ladleful at a time, allowing the rice to absorb the liquid before adding more and stirring all the time. After 20–30 minutes the rice should be golden yellow and creamy, and *al dente* when tested.

saffron

pumpkin

white wine

onion

garlic

marjoram

Parmesan

arborio rice

pistachios

2 Heat the oil in a large saucepan. Add the onion and garlic and cook gently for about 5 minutes until softened. Add the rice and pumpkin and cook for a few more minutes until the rice looks transparent.

3 Pour in the wine and allow it to bubble hard. When it is absorbed add ¼ of the stock and the infused saffron and liquid. Stir constantly until all the liquid is absorbed.

5 Stir in the Parmesan cheese, cover the pan and leave to stand for 5 minutes.

6 To finish, stir in the pistachios and marjoram or oregano. Season to taste with a little salt, nutmeg and pepper, and scatter over a few extra marjoram or oregano leaves.

COOK'S TIP
Italian arborio rice must be used to make an authentic risotto. Choose unpolished white arborio as it contains more starch.

Wild Rice Rösti with Carrot and Orange Purée

Rösti is a traditional dish from Switzerland. This variation has the extra nuttiness of wild rice and a bright simple sauce as a fresh accompaniment.

Serves 6

INGREDIENTS
50 g/2 oz/½ cup wild rice
900 g/2 lb large potatoes
45 ml/3 tbsp walnut oil
5 ml/1 tsp yellow mustard seeds
1 onion, coarsely grated and drained
    in a sieve
30 ml/2 tbsp fresh thyme leaves
salt and freshly ground black pepper

FOR THE PURÉE
350 g/12 oz carrots, peeled and
    roughly chopped
rind and juice of 1 large orange

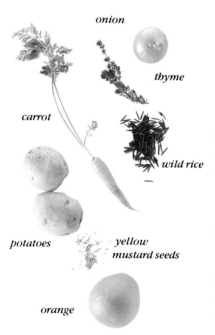

onion

thyme

carrot

wild rice

potatoes

yellow mustard seeds

orange

1 For the purée, place the carrots in a pan, cover with cold water and add 2 pieces of orange rind. Bring to the boil and cook for 10 minutes or until tender. Drain well and discard the rind.

2 Purée the mixture in a blender with 60 ml/4 tbsp of the orange juice. Return to the pan to reheat.

3 Place the wild rice in a clean pan and cover with water. Bring to the boil and cook for 30–40 minutes, until the rice is just starting to split, but still crunchy. Drain the rice.

4 Scrub the potatoes, place in a large pan and cover with cold water. Bring to the boil and cook for 10–15 minutes until just tender. Drain well and leave to cool slightly. When the potatoes are cool, peel and coarsely grate them into a large bowl. Add the cooked rice.

5 Heat 30 ml/2 tbsp of the walnut oil in a non-stick frying pan and add the mustard seeds. When they start to pop, add the onion and cook gently for 5 minutes until softened. Add to the bowl of potato and rice, together with the thyme, and mix thoroughly. Season to taste with salt and pepper.

6 Heat the remaining oil in the frying pan and add the potato mixture. Press down well and cook for 10 minutes or until golden brown. Cover the pan with a plate and flip over, then slide the rösti back into the pan for another 10 minutes to cook the other side. Serve with the reheated carrot and orange purée.

Thai Fragrant Rice

A lovely, soft, fluffy rice dish, perfumed with fresh lemon grass.

Serves 4

INGREDIENTS
1 piece of lemon grass
2 limes
225 g/8 oz/1 cup brown basmati rice
15 ml/1 tbsp olive oil
1 onion, chopped
2.5 cm/1 in piece of fresh ginger root, peeled and finely chopped
7.5 ml/1½ tsp coriander seeds
7.5 ml/1½ tsp cumin seeds
700 ml/1¼ pints/3 cups vegetable stock
60 ml/4 tbsp chopped fresh coriander
lime wedges, to serve

onion

lime

ginger

lemon grass

coriander seeds

basmati rice

cumin seeds

coriander

1 Finely chop the lemon grass.

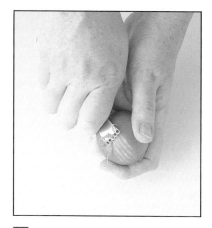

2 Remove the zest from the limes using a zester or fine grater.

3 Rinse the rice in plenty of cold water until the water runs clear. Drain through a sieve.

4 Heat the oil in a large pan and add the onion, spices, lemon grass and lime zest and cook gently for 2–3 minutes.

5 Add the rice and cook for another minute, then add the stock and bring to the boil. Reduce the heat to very low and cover the pan. Cook gently for 30 minutes then check the rice. If it is still crunchy, cover the pan again and leave for a further 3–5 minutes. Remove from the heat.

6 Stir in the fresh coriander, fluff up the grains, cover and leave for 10 minutes. Serve with lime wedges.

COOK'S TIP

Other varieties of rice, such as white basmati or long grain, can be used for this dish but you will need to adjust the cooking times accordingly.

Cannellini Bean Pureé with Grilled Radicchio

The slightly bitter flavours of the radicchio and chicory make a wonderful marriage with the creamy citrus bean purée.

Serves 4

INGREDIENTS
1 × 400 g/14 oz can cannellini beans
45 ml/3 tbsp low-fat fromage blanc
finely grated zest, rind and juice of 1
    large orange
15 ml/1 tbsp finely chopped fresh
    rosemary
4 heads of chicory
2 medium radicchio
15 ml/1 tbsp walnut oil

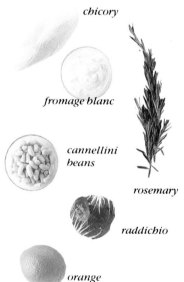

chicory

fromage blanc

cannellini
beans

rosemary

raddichio

orange

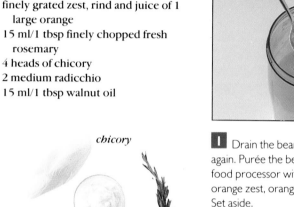

1 Drain the beans, rinse, and drain again. Purée the beans in a blender or food processor with the fromage blanc, orange zest, orange juice and rosemary. Set aside.

2 Cut the chicory in half lengthwise.

3 Cut each radicchio into 8 wedges

4 Lay out the chicory and radicchio on a baking tray and brush with walnut oil. Grill for 2–3 minutes. Serve with the puree and scatter over the orange rind.

COOK'S TIP
Other suitable beans to use are haricot, mung or broad beans.

Tabbouleh with Fennel and Pomegranate

A fresh salad originating in the Middle East, with the added crunchiness of fennel and sweet pomegranate seeds. It is perfect for a summer lunch.

Serves 6

INGREDIENTS
225 g/8 oz/1 cup bulgur wheat
2 fennel bulbs
1 small fresh red chilli, seeded and
    finely chopped
1 celery stick, finely sliced
30 ml/2 tbsp olive oil
finely grated rind and juice of 2
    lemons
6–8 spring onions, chopped
90 ml/6 tbsp chopped fresh mint
90 ml/6 tbsp chopped fresh parsley
1 pomegranate, seeds removed
salt and freshly ground black pepper

lemon

red chilli

celery

bulgur wheat

spring onion

fennel

pomegranate

parsley

mint

1 Place the bulgur wheat in a bowl and pour over enough cold water to cover. Leave to stand for 30 minutes.

2 Drain the wheat through a sieve, pressing out any excess water using a spoon.

3 Halve the fennel bulbs and cut into very fine slices.

4 Mix all the remaining ingredients together, including the soaked bulgur wheat and fennel. Season well, cover, and set aside for 30 minutes before serving.

Sweet Vegetable Couscous

A wonderful combination of sweet vegetables and spices, this makes a substantial winter dish.

Serves 4–6

INGREDIENTS

1 generous pinch of saffron threads
45 ml/3 tbsp boiling water
15 ml/1 tbsp olive oil
1 red onion, sliced
2 garlic cloves crushed
1–2 fresh red chillies, seeded and
  finely chopped
2.5 ml/½ tsp ground ginger
2.5 ml/½ tsp ground cinnamon
1 × 400 g/14 oz can chopped
  tomatoes
300 ml/½ pint/1¼ cups vegetable
  stock or water
4 medium carrots, peeled and cut into
  5 mm/¼ in slices
2 medium turnips, peeled and cut into
  2 cm/¾ in cubes
450 g/1 lb sweet potatoes, peeled and
  cut into 2 cm/¾ in cubes
75 g/3 oz/⅓ cup raisins
2 medium courgettes, cut into 5 mm/
  ¼ in slices
1 × 400 g/14 oz can chick-peas,
  drained and rinsed
45 ml/3 tbsp chopped fresh parsley
45 ml/3 tbsp chopped fresh coriander
450 g/1 lb quick-cook couscous

1 Leave the saffron to infuse in the boiling water.

2 Heat the oil in a large saucepan. Add the onion, garlic and chillies and cook gently for 5 minutes.

3 Add the ground ginger and cinnamon and cook for a further 1–2 minutes.

4 Add the tomatoes, stock or water, infused saffron and liquid, carrots, turnips, sweet potatoes and raisins, cover and simmer for 25 minutes.

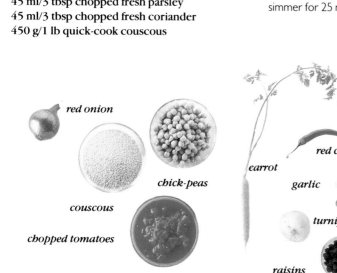

red onion

chick-peas

couscous

chopped tomatoes

courgette

carrot

red chilli

garlic

turnip

raisins

sweet potato

5 Add the courgettes, chick-peas, parsley and coriander and cook for another 10 minutes.

6 Meanwhile prepare the couscous following the packet instructions and serve with the vegetables.

Lemon and Ginger Spicy Beans

An extremely quick delicious meal, made with canned beans for speed. You probably won't need extra salt as canned beans tend to be already salted.

Serves 4

INGREDIENTS

5 cm/2 in piece fresh ginger root, peeled and roughly chopped
3 garlic cloves, roughly chopped
250 ml/8 fl oz/1 cup cold water
15 ml/1 tbsp sunflower oil
1 large onion, thinly sliced
1 fresh red chilli, seeded and finely chopped
¼ tsp cayenne pepper
10 ml/2 tsp ground cumin
5 ml/1 tsp ground coriander
½ tsp ground turmeric
30 ml/2 tbsp lemon juice
75 g/3 oz/⅓ cup chopped fresh coriander
1 × 400 g/14 oz can black-eyed beans, drained and rinsed
1 × 400 g/14 oz can aduki beans, drained and rinsed
1 × 400 g/14 oz can haricot beans, drained and rinsed
freshly ground black pepper

garlic
red chilli
aduki beans
ginger
black-eyed beans
ground coriander
ground turmeric
ground cumin
haricot beans
onion

1 Place the ginger, garlic and 60 ml/4 tbsp of the cold water in a blender and mix until smooth.

2 Heat the oil in a pan. Add the onion and chilli and cook gently for 5 minutes until softened.

3 Add the cayenne pepper, cumin, ground coriander and turmeric and stir-fry for 1 minute.

4 Stir in the ginger and garlic paste from the blender and cook for another minute.

5 Add the remaining water, lemon juice and fresh coriander, stir well and bring to the boil. Cover the pan tightly and cook for 5 minutes.

6 Add all the beans and cook for a further 5–10 minutes. Season with pepper and serve.

Green Lentil and Cabbage Salad

This warm crunchy salad makes a satisfying meal if served with crusty French bread or wholemeal rolls.

Serves 4–6

INGREDIENTS
225 g/8 oz/1 cup puy lentils
1.3 litres/2¼ pints/6 cups cold water
1 garlic clove
1 bay leaf
1 small onion, peeled and studded
  with 2 cloves
15 ml/1 tbsp olive oil
1 red onion, finely sliced
2 garlic cloves, crushed
15 ml/1 tbsp thyme leaves
350 g/12 oz cabbage, finely shredded
finely grated rind and juice of 1 lemon
15 ml/1 tbsp raspberry vinegar
salt and freshly ground black pepper

thyme

cabbage

onion

red onion

bay leaf

lemon

garlic

cloves

peppercorns

1 Rinse the lentils in cold water and place in a large pan with the water, peeled garlic clove, bay leaf and clove-studded onion. Bring to the boil and cook for 10 minutes. Reduce the heat, cover the pan and simmer gently for 15–20 minutes. Drain and remove the onion, garlic and bay leaf.

2 Heat the oil in a large pan. Add the red onion, garlic and thyme and cook for 5 minutes until softened.

3 Add the cabbage and cook for 3–5 minutes until just cooked but still crunchy.

4 Stir in the cooked lentils, lemon rind and juice and the raspberry vinegar. Season to taste and serve.

Polenta and Baked Tomatoes

A staple of northern Italy, polenta is a nourishing, filling food, served here with a delicious fresh tomato and olive topping.

Serves 4–6

INGREDIENTS
2 litres/3½ pints/9 cups water
500 g/1¼ lb quick-cook polenta
12 large ripe plum tomatoes, sliced
4 garlic cloves, thinly sliced
30 ml/2 tbsp chopped fresh oregano
 or marjoram
115 g/4 oz/½ cup black olives, pitted
salt and freshly ground black pepper
30 ml/2 tbsp olive oil

black olives

marjoram

plum tomatoes

garlic

oregano

polenta

1 Place the water in a large saucepan and bring to the boil. Whisk in the polenta and simmer for 5 minutes.

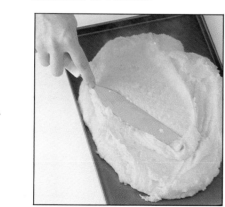

2 Remove the pan from the heat and pour the polenta into a 23 cm × 33 cm/ 9 in × 13 in Swiss roll tin. Smooth out the surface with a palette knife until level, and leave to cool.

3 Preheat the oven to 180°C/350°F/ Gas 4. With a 7.5 cm/3 in round pastry cutter, stamp out 12 rounds of polenta. Lay them so that they slightly overlap in a lightly oiled ovenproof dish.

4 Layer the tomatoes, garlic, oregano or marjoram and olives on top of the polenta, seasoning the layers as you go. Sprinkle with the olive oil, and bake uncovered for 30–35 minutes. Serve immediately.

French Bread Pizzas with Artichokes

Crunchy French bread makes an ideal base for these quick pizzas.

Serves 4

INGREDIENTS

15 ml/1 tbsp sunflower oil
1 onion, chopped
1 green pepper, seeded and
  chopped
200 g/7 oz can chopped tomatoes
15 ml/1 tbsp tomato purée
½ French stick
400 g/14 oz can artichoke
  hearts, drained
115 g/4 oz mozzarella cheese, sliced
15 ml/1 tbsp poppy seeds
salt and freshly ground black pepper

mozzarella cheese

French stick

tomato purée

chopped tomatoes

green pepper

poppy seeds

onion

artichoke hearts

1 Heat the oil in a frying pan. Add the chopped onion and pepper and cook for 4 minutes until just softened.

2 Stir in the chopped tomatoes and tomato purée. Cook for 4 minutes. Remove from the heat and add salt and pepper to taste.

3 Cut the piece of French stick in half lengthways. Cut each half in four to give eight pieces in all.

4 Spoon a little of the pepper and tomato mixture over each piece of bread. Preheat the grill.

5 Slice the artichoke hearts. Arrange them on top of the pepper and tomato mixture. Cover with the mozzarella slices and sprinkle with the poppy seeds.

6 Arrange the French bread pizzas on a rack over a grill pan and grill for 6–8 minutes until the cheese melts and is beginning to brown. Serve at once.

Courgette and Walnut Loaf

Cardamom seeds impart their distinctive aroma to this loaf. Serve spread with ricotta and honey for a delicious snack.

Makes 1 loaf

INGREDIENTS
3 × size 3 eggs
75 g/3 oz/⅓ cup light muscovado sugar
100 ml/4 fl oz/½ cup sunflower oil
225 g/8 oz/2 cups wholemeal flour
5 ml/1 tsp baking powder
5 ml/1 tsp bicarbonate of soda
5 ml/1 tsp ground cinnamon
3 ml/¾ tsp ground allspice
7.5 ml/½ tbsp green cardamoms, seeds removed and crushed
150 g/5 oz courgette, coarsely grated
115 g/4 oz/½ cup walnuts, chopped
50 g/2 oz/¼ cup sunflower seeds

courgettes

walnuts

egg

sunflower oil

muscovado sugar

wholemeal flour

sunflower seeds

cardamom pods

1 Preheat the oven to 180°C/350°F/ Gas 4. Line the base and sides of a 900 g/ 2 lb loaf tin with non-stick baking paper.

2 Beat the eggs and sugar together and gradually add the oil.

3 Sift the flour into a bowl together with the baking powder, bicarbonate of soda, cinnamon and allspice.

4 Mix into the egg mixture with the rest of the ingredients, reserving 15 g/1 tbsp of the sunflower seeds for the top.

5 Spoon into the loaf tin, level off the top, and sprinkle with the reserved sunflower seeds.

6 Bake for 1 hour or until a skewer inserted in the centre comes out clean. Leave to cool slightly before turning out onto a wire rack to cool completely.

Red Pepper and Watercress Filo Parcels

Peppery watercress combines well with sweet red pepper in these crisp little parcels.

Makes 8

INGREDIENTS
3 red peppers
175 g/6 oz watercress
225 g/8 oz/1 cup ricotta cheese
50 g/2 oz/¼ cup blanched almonds,
  toasted and chopped
salt and freshly ground black pepper
8 sheets of filo pastry
30 ml/2 tbsp olive oil

ricotta

red pepper

watercress

almonds

filo pastry

1 Preheat the oven to 190°C/375°F/Gas 5. Place the peppers under a hot grill until blistered and charred. Place in a plastic bag. When cool enough to handle peel, seed and pat dry on kitchen paper.

2 Place the peppers and watercress in a food processor and pulse until coarsely chopped. Spoon into a bowl.

3 Mix in the ricotta and almonds, and season to taste.

4 Working with 1 sheet of filo pastry at a time, cut out 2 × 18 cm/7 in and 2 × 5 cm/2 in squares from each sheet. Brush 1 large square with a little olive oil and place a second large square at an angle of 90 degrees to form a star shape.

5 Place 1 of the small squares in the centre of the star shape, brush lightly with oil and top with a second small square.

6 Top with ⅛ of the red pepper mixture. Bring the edges together to form a purse shape and twist to seal. Place on a lightly greased baking sheet and cook for 25–30 minutes until golden.

Sage Soda Bread

This wonderful loaf, quite unlike bread made with yeast, has a velvety texture and a powerful sage aroma.

Makes 1 loaf

INGREDIENTS
225 g/8 oz/2 cups wholemeal flour
115 g/4 oz/1 cup strong white flour
2.5 ml/½ tsp salt
5 ml/1 tsp bicarbonate of soda
30 ml/2 tbsp shredded fresh sage
300–450 ml/½–¾ pint/1¼–1¾
   cups buttermilk

white flour

wholemeal flour

sage

buttermilk

COOK'S TIP

As an alternative to the sage, try using finely chopped rosemary or thyme.

1 Preheat the oven to 220°C/425°F/ Gas 7. Sift the dry ingredients into a bowl.

2 Stir in the sage and add enough buttermilk to make a soft dough.

3 Shape the dough into a round loaf and place on a lightly oiled baking sheet.

4 Cut a deep cross in the top. Bake in the oven for 40 minutes until the loaf is well risen and sounds hollow when tapped on the bottom. Leave to cool on a wire rack.

Mini Pizzas

For a quick supper dish try these delicious little pizzas made with fresh and sun-dried tomatoes.

Makes 4

INGREDIENTS
1 × 150 g/5 oz packet pizza mix
8 halves sun-dried tomatoes in olive oil, drained
50 g/2 oz/½ cup black olives, pitted
225 g/8 oz ripe tomatoes, sliced
50 g/2 oz/¼ cup goat's cheese
30 ml/2 tbsp fresh basil leaves

basil

tomatoes

sun-dried tomatoes

black olives

goat's cheese

1 Preheat the oven to 200°C/400°F/Gas 6. Make up the pizza base following the instructions on the side of the packet.

2 Divide the dough into 4 and roll each piece out to a 13 cm/5 in disc. Place on a lightly oiled baking sheet.

COOK'S TIP

You could use loose sun-dried tomatoes (preserved without oil) instead. Leave in a bowl of warm water for 10–15 minutes to soften, drain and blend with the olives.

3 Place the sun-dried tomatoes and olives in a blender or food processor and blend until smooth. Spread the mixture evenly over the pizza bases.

4 Top with the tomato slices and crumble over the goat's cheese. Bake for 10–15 minutes. Sprinkle with the fresh basil and serve.

Aubergine, Shallot and Sun-dried Tomato Calzone

Aubergines, shallots and sun-dried tomatoes make an unusual filling for calzone. Add more or less red chilli flakes, depending on personal taste.

Serves 2

INGREDIENTS
45 ml/3 tbsp olive oil
3 shallots, chopped
4 baby aubergines
1 garlic clove, chopped
50 g/2 oz sun-dried tomatoes
  in oil, chopped
1.25 ml/¼ tsp dried red chilli flakes
10 ml/2 tsp chopped fresh thyme
1 packet pizza dough mix
75 g/3 oz mozzarella, cubed
salt and ground black pepper
15–30 ml/1–2 tbsp freshly grated
  Parmesan, to serve

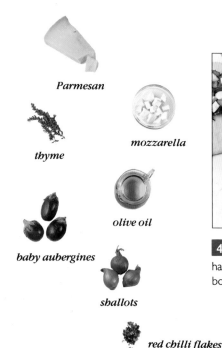

Parmesan

thyme

mozzarella

olive oil

baby aubergines

shallots

red chilli flakes

1 Preheat the oven to 220°C/425°F/ Gas 7. Trim the aubergines, then cut into small cubes.

2 Cook the shallots until soft in a frying pan. Add the aubergines, garlic, sun-dried tomatoes, red chilli flakes, thyme and seasoning. Cook for 4–5 minutes, stirring frequently, until the aubergine is beginning to soften.

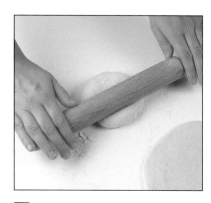

3 Make the dough according to the directions on the packet. Divide the dough in half and roll out each piece on a lightly floured surface to an 18 cm/7 in circle.

4 Spread the aubergine mixture over half of each circle, leaving a 2.5 cm/1 in border, then scatter over the mozzarella.

5 Dampen the edges with water, then fold over the other half of dough to enclose the filling. Press the edges firmly together to seal. Place on two greased baking sheets.

6 Brush with half the remaining oil and make a small hole in the top of each to allow the steam to escape. Bake for 15–20 minutes until golden. Remove from the oven and brush with the remaining oil. Sprinkle over the Parmesan and serve immediately.

Parsnip and Pecan Gougères with Watercress and Rocket Sauce

These scrumptious nutty puffs conceal a surprisingly sweet parsnip centre.

Makes 18

INGREDIENTS
115 g/4 oz/½ cup butter
300 ml/½ pint/1¼ cups water
75 g/3 oz/¾ cup plain flour
50 g/2 oz/½ cup wholemeal flour
3 × size 3 eggs, beaten
25 g/1 oz Cheddar cheese, grated
pinch of cayenne pepper or paprika
75 g/3 oz/⅔ cup pecans, chopped
1 medium parsnip, cut into
   18 × 2 cm/¾ in pieces
15 ml/1 tbsp skimmed milk
10 ml/2 tsp sesame seeds

FOR THE SAUCE
150 g/5 oz watercress, trimmed
150 g/5 oz rocket, trimmed
175 ml/6 fl oz/¾ cup low-fat yogurt
salt, grated nutmeg and freshly ground
   black pepper
watercress sprigs, to garnish

1 Preheat the oven to 200°C/400°F/ Gas 6. Place the butter and water in a pan. Bring to the boil and add all the flour in one go. Beat vigorously until the mixture leaves the sides of the pan and forms a ball. Remove from heat and allow the mixture to cool slightly. Beat in the eggs a little at a time until the mixture is shiny and soft enough to fall gently from a spoon.

2 Beat in the Cheddar, cayenne pepper or paprika and the chopped pecans.

3 Lightly grease a baking sheet and drop onto it 18 heaped tablespoons of the mixture. Place a piece of parsnip on each and top with another heaped tablespoon of the mixture.

4 Brush the gougères with a little milk and sprinkle with sesame seeds. Bake in the oven for 25–30 minutes until firm and golden.

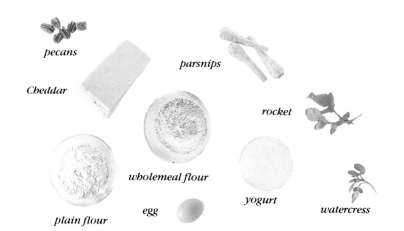

pecans

Cheddar

parsnips

rocket

wholemeal flour

egg

yogurt

watercress

plain flour

5 Meanwhile make the sauce. Bring a pan of water to the boil and blanch the watercress and rocket for 2–3 minutes. Drain and immediately refresh in cold water. Drain well and chop.

6 Purée the watercress and rocket in a blender or food processor with the yogurt until smooth. Season to taste with salt, nutmeg and freshly ground black pepper. To reheat, place the sauce in a bowl over a gently simmering pan of hot water and heat gently, taking care not to let the sauce curdle. Garnish with watercress.

Tomato Breadsticks

Once you've tried this simple recipe you'll never buy manufactured breadsticks again. Serve with aperitifs with a dip or with cheese to end a meal.

Makes 16

INGREDIENTS
225 g/8 oz/2 cups plain flour
2.5 ml/½ tsp salt
7.5 ml/½ tbsp easy-blend dry yeast
5 ml/1 tsp honey
5 ml/1 tsp olive oil
150 ml/¼ pint/⅔ cup warm water
6 halves sun-dried tomatoes in olive
   oil, drained and chopped
15 ml/1 tbsp skimmed milk
10 ml/2 tsp poppy seeds

plain flour

sun-dried tomatoes

honey

yeast

poppy seeds

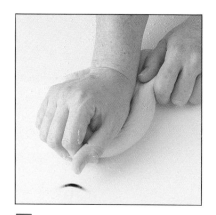

1 Place the flour, salt and yeast in a food processor. Add the honey and olive oil and, with the machine running, gradually pour in the water (you may not need it all as flours vary). Stop adding water as soon as the dough starts to cling together. Process for 1 minute more.

2 Turn out the dough onto a floured board and knead for 3–4 minutes until springy and smooth. Knead in the chopped sun-dried tomatoes. Form into a ball and place in a lightly oiled bowl. Leave to rise for 5 minutes.

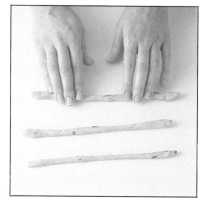

3 Preheat the oven to 150°C/300°F/ Gas 2. Divide the dough into 16 pieces and roll each piece into a 28 cm × 1 cm/ 11 in × ½ in long stick. Place on a lightly oiled baking sheet and leave to rise in a warm place for 15 minutes.

4 Brush the sticks with milk and sprinkle with poppy seeds. Bake for 30 minutes. Leave to cool on a wire rack.

Oatmeal Tartlets with Minted Houmus

Serve these wholesome little tartlets with a crisp salad of cos lettuce.

Serves 6

INGREDIENTS

225 g/8 oz/1½ cups medium oatmeal
2.5 ml/½ tsp bicarbonate of soda
5 ml/1 tsp salt
25g/1 oz/2 tbsp butter
1 egg yolk
30 ml/2 tbsp skimmed milk
1 × 400 g/14 oz can chick-peas,
   rinsed and drained
juice of 1–2 lemons
350 g/12 oz/1½ cups low-fat fromage
   blanc
60 ml/4 tbsp tahini
freshly ground black pepper
45 ml/3 tbsp chopped fresh mint
25 g/1 oz/2 tbsp pumpkin seeds
paprika, for dusting

tahini

pumpkin seeds

fromage blanc

chick-peas

oatmeal

mint

lemon

1 Preheat the oven to 160°C/325°F/ Gas 3. Mix together the oatmeal, bicarbonate of soda and salt in a large bowl. Rub in the butter until the mixture resembles fine breadcrumbs. Stir in the egg yolk and add the milk if the mixture seems too dry.

2 Press into 6 × 9 cm/3½ in tartlet tins. Bake for 25–30 minutes. Allow to cool.

3 Purée the chick-peas, the juice of 1 lemon, fromage blanc and tahini in a food processor until smooth. Spoon into a bowl and season with black pepper and more lemon juice to taste. Stir in the chopped mint. Divide between the tartlet moulds, sprinkle with pumpkin seeds and dust with paprika.

Saffron Focaccia

A dazzling yellow bread that is light in texture and distinctive in flavour.

Makes 1 loaf

INGREDIENTS
pinch of saffron threads
150 ml/¼ pint/⅔ cup boiling water
225 g/8 oz/2 cups plain flour
2.5 ml/½ tsp salt
5 ml/1 tsp easy-blend dry yeast
15 ml/1 tbsp olive oil

FOR THE TOPPING
2 garlic cloves, sliced
1 red onion, cut into thin wedges
rosemary sprigs
12 black olives, pitted and coarsely
    chopped
15 ml/1 tbsp olive oil

flour

garlic

rosemary

red onion

olives

saffron

yeast

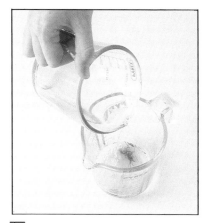

1 Place the saffron in a heatproof jug and pour on the boiling water. Leave to stand and infuse until lukewarm.

2 Place the flour, salt, yeast and olive oil in a food processor. Turn on and gradually add the saffron and its liquid. Process until the dough forms into a ball.

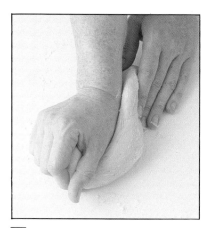

3 Turn onto a floured board and knead for 10–15 minutes. Place in a bowl, cover and leave to rise for 30–40 minutes until doubled in size.

4 Punch down the risen dough on a lightly floured surface and roll out into an oval shape, 1 cm/½ in thick. Place on a lightly greased baking tray and leave to rise for 20–30 minutes.

5 Preheat the oven to 200°C/400°F/Gas 6. Use your fingers to press small indentations all over the surface of the focaccia.

6 Cover with the topping ingredients, brush lightly with olive oil, and bake for 25 minutes or until the loaf sounds hollow when tapped on the bottom. Leave to cool on a wire rack.

Date and Apple Muffins

You will only need one or two of these wholesome muffins per person as they are very filling.

Makes 12

INGREDIENTS

150 g/5 oz/1¼ cups self-raising
   wholemeal flour
150 g/5 oz/1¼ cups self-raising
   white flour
5 ml/1 tsp ground cinnamon
5 ml/1 tsp baking powder
25 g/1 oz/2 tbsp soft margarine
75 g/3 oz/½ cup light muscovado
   sugar
1 eating apple
250 ml/8 fl oz/1 cup apple juice
30 ml/2 tbsp pear and apple spread
1 egg, lightly beaten
75 g/3 oz/½ cup chopped dates
15 ml/1 tbsp chopped pecan nuts

chopped dates — *egg* — *pecan nuts* — *self-raising wholemeal flour* — *ground cinnamon* — *muscovado sugar*

self-raising white flour — *apple juice* — *soft margarine* — *pear and apple spread* — *eating apple*

baking powder

1 Preheat the oven to 200°C/400°F/Gas 6. Arrange 12 paper cases in a deep muffin tin. Put the wholemeal flour in a mixing bowl. Sift in the white flour with the cinnamon and baking powder. Rub in the margarine until the mixture resembles breadcrumbs, then stir in the muscovado sugar.

2 Quarter and core the apple, chop the flesh finely and set aside. Stir a little of the apple juice with the pear and apple spread until smooth. Mix in the remaining juice, then add to the rubbed-in mixture with the egg. Add the chopped apple to the bowl with the dates. Mix quickly until just combined.

3 Divide the mixture among the muffin cases.

4 Sprinkle with the chopped pecan nuts. Bake the muffins for 20–25 minutes until golden brown and firm in the middle. Remove to a wire rack and serve while still warm.

Raspberry Muffins

These American muffins are made using baking powder and low fat buttermilk, giving them a light and spongy texture. They are delicious to eat at any time of day.

Makes 10–12

INGREDIENTS
275 g/10 oz/2½ cups plain flour
15 ml/1 tbsp baking powder
115 g/4 oz/½ cup caster sugar
1 egg
250 ml/8 fl oz/1 cup buttermilk
60 ml/4 tbsp sunflower oil
150 g/5 oz/1 cup raspberries

egg

buttermilk

sunflower oil

caster sugar

baking powder

plain flour

raspberries

1 Preheat the oven to 200°C/400°F/Gas 6. Arrange 12 paper cases in a deep muffin tin. Sift the flour and baking powder into a mixing bowl, stir in the sugar, then make a well in the centre.

2 Mix the egg, buttermilk and sunflower oil together in a bowl, pour into the flour mixture and mix quickly until just combined.

3 Add the raspberries and lightly fold in with a metal spoon. Spoon the mixture into the paper cases to within a third of the top.

4 Bake the muffins for 20–25 minutes until golden brown and firm in the middle. Transfer to a wire rack and serve warm or cold.

 # INDEX

INDEX